The Power of Fear

How to defeat its authority over your life through Faith!

Soraya F. Présumé Calixte, PhD.

ISBN: 1547259612
ISBN 13: 9781547259618
LCCN Imprint Name : Soraya Media Group Inc.

spacesupport.org

ACKNOWLEDGMENTS

I crave to thank God, my Savior and Redeemer, who steered me to where I am today precisely where I belong, in His promise for my life. To write this book, it took the amazing strength and support of my loving husband, Prosper Calixte, who has been reminding me to take a break while supporting me through sleepless nights and long work hours. It also took the driving force of my two exceptional gifts from above, my dear children, Esther (Gabby) and Joshua, who would stop by my room to remind me how much they love me. I love you more my precious jewels. Through my journey, I met and fellowshipped with some amazing women of God. Their guidance and support through this long journey kept me growing and going. Thanks to my spiritual mother and advisor, the late Pastor Dr. Mona Joseph, who agreed on the mandate to hold my hands and to walk with me in faith, regardless of the challenges been faced. To my friends, beautiful sisters in Christ, Nicole Delva, Marceléne Claude, Owepatrice Gaillard women of faith, prayer warriors, and all the Sentinels.

To my mother Carole Paul, who took the time to bring me to the church at a very tender age; she helped me understand the meaning of learning while supporting me to the very best of her knowledge. To Djenane Sajous and family, who opened their hearts and school to make sure that education is one thing that I did not lack, some heartfelt thanks. I am grateful to my stunning and best friend Ariège Alcé and her family, who adopted me unconditionally. I thank all the preachers from the NJEBChurch who prepare those powerful sermons. Finally, to my friend and sisters in Christ, Maria Pina, Aminah Pilgrim, Stephanie Présumé, and Zouzou for their editing support. My colleagues, Angela Leite, Yvonne Winston, Amelia Falavinha, my little brother; Jean Alain Présumé, Mrs. Caruso, Marie Laurent, who in one way or the other supported me with this book. I am grateful to you. To God be the glory!

TABLE OF CONTENTS

CHAPTER XIII

M. FAITH CAN PULL YOU THROUGH... pg. 92

CHAPTER XIV

AUTHOR'S VISIONS & SHARED TESTIMONIES

Who can go through life without experiencing fear? As I look back, I recall some frightful events in my life. Experiencing two civil wars from the age of 10 through 12 certainly instilled fear into me. Fear can be debilitating, and how many of us struggle with it throughout our lives? As I read this book, I couldn't help but wonder the pervasiveness of this issue. This book is so relevant, important, practical, and it benefits to us all.

The Power of Fear is a timely and refreshing look at a topic that keeps many of us, believers and nonbelievers alike, in bondage. It reads like an honest and intimate conversation with a friend at a coffee shop. Although, the topic is heavy and dense, the author manages to leave us with the hope and expectation that this too can and shall be overcome. All the while, guiding us to numerous biblical examples that attest to how fear can be conquered. In addition, this book sensitively takes us on a journey via the testimonies of individuals from whom we can not only empathize, but also learn. I honor each and every one of their stories. The author, in a clever way, parallels biblical examples of triumph to our practical experiences so that we too, by applying the same principles, can also win the same battle.

Since none of us are immune from this pervasive spirit, it is imperative that one arm oneself. The Power of Fear not only serves as a pertinent read but also as a reference to the many scriptural passages one should study when dealing with the subject of fear. Where better to look to than the bible in which we find all instruction to living a victorious life?

Thank you, Soraya, for venturing into this God-led journey and condensing this information so that more people can gain knowledge of the One who can truly liberate us from the spirit of fear. In this way, we can live life more abundantly!

_ *Maria Pina*

Dr. Présumé Calixte has created a powerful tool that simultaneously delivers God's word and offers a practical guide for how to grow and apply one's faith in the midst of various fears. My own faith was amplified through reading this book. Her voice is our gift. She is precisely the kind of strong witness and evangelist that we need for our present time.

Dr. Aminah Pilgrim

Filled with practical and personal testimonies, this book gives us hope, bolster our faith and provides inspirational advices to help us walk by faith and not by sight.

Ambiancefm.com

Soraya's book is excellent, very thorough and it will be a very good addition and complement to some of the other work on this topic. She delivered some inspiring insights that will help others in their journey of faith. Be Blessed.

Sandy Coelho

INTRODUCTION

As we order this book or any item online or over the phone, we agree to believe that someone we cannot see on the other end would send us something when we order it. Hence, there is nothing silly when you check your mailbox with the expectation it will be there. In this book, we will discover that through personal life experiences, and through the experiences of other men and women in the Bible despite the trials and tribulations, we are able to conquer our fears and live a faithful and prosperous life.

It was necessary to write this book for those of you who are waiting to digest these inspiring words that were given to me from above. This book is a testimony of faith. There is a mélange of challenges of fear, despair, and deception. However, here you will read a message of hope, courage, desire, determination, discipline, and perseverance. This book is written as a collection of testimonies that lead to freedom when we keep our eyes on God. Regardless of the situation and judgment, we need to remind ourselves that we are not alone. He has been watching over us before we even came into existence. As His Word states, "Before I formed you in the womb I knew you before you were born I set you apart; I appointed you as a prophet to the nations" (Jeremiah 1:5).

By relying and depending on God's Word, we can move the mountains in our daily lives and reach hope, maturity, peace, and faith while building our character. Many of you may feel overwhelmed as your eyes are decoding each Word. One thing that we should know for sure is that hope is just around the corner, and we must not give up. If it is true that "*What doesn't kill you makes you stronger,*" then in God's kingdom, the victory is always ours, and we need to learn the skills to claim what is rightfully ours. Through the blood of Jesus, we are not bitter but better, and we are not victims but conquerors.

Throughout the Bible, we read stories, and in our current life situations, we will analyze the connections, if any between fear and faith. Which one prevails in our daily lives? If you have been under the bondage of fear, doubt, and negativity, be ready to experience the power of a simple belief in the Great I Am. It is important that our thoughts connect with the Word of God, so we can reach that realm of grace that is up for grabs.

In this book, my intention is to demonstrate how we can cultivate faith to conquer negative fears when we know who we are in God.

The Bible states that "Faith comes by hearing and hearing by the Word of God" (Hebrews 11:1). But we may not understand at times the ways and means of implementing faith once we acquire it. The Bible says "If you have faith as small as a mustard seed, you can say to this mountain, move from here to there, and it will move. Nothing will be impossible for you" (Matthew 17:20). Understanding the faith that can move mountains would help us manage any type of fear. The best way to overcome any battle is through faith. Faith that does not wavers, faith that is engrained in God and total surrender and belief in His Word. Therefore, we must know God and have a relationship with Him to conquer fear. Jesus reminded, "Behold, I give you the authority to trample on serpents and scorpions, and over all the power of the enemy, and nothing shall by any means hurt you" (Luke 10:19). Let us discover the true and illusory nature of fear. Let us build our faith while triumphing over our minds, thoughts, and surrounding doubts in our daily lives. We are always exercising faith whether we realize it or not.

CHAPTER I
A. UNDERSTANDING FEAR

When one is trying to share evidence, it is not only important to be well informed but even more importantly to have a solid point of reference. Hence, in this journey of battling fear to conquer faith, one needs to grasp a true understanding and the accurate nature of those two concepts. Fear and faith may be antagonistic to one another, but one usually takes over the other. Per Proverbs (9:10), "The fear of God is the beginning of wisdom." It is important to point out the fear of the Lord which has to do with respect, reverence, and honor. Generally, we tend to act out our own warped wisdom, which is more often corrupted by our own biases. For example, a young person may naively choose a spouse based on their own knowledge and understanding without the wisdom and input from their parents. Where there is wisdom, chaos can easily be avoided, and knowledge is required for almost every endeavor that one wishes to tackle. If this couple is not afraid, has the necessary wisdom and their relationship is based on the Word, they are most likely to succeed in their marriage. Fear can be an unswerving darkness when we want to accomplish anything in life. Therefore, we need wisdom to intercede it and not intimidation.

"By wisdom the Lord laid the earth's foundations, by understanding he set the heavens in place; by his knowledge, the deeps were divided" (Proverbs 3:19-20). It is God who gives knowledge and wisdom. Therefore, when someone does not know God, this person is lost. If one does not know who they are and to whom they belong, fear is able to dominate over their lives. Overall, fear can be a positive or a negative experience depending on how it is managed or dealt with.

1

1. Definition of Fear

Fear is the one thing that we can say is universal; nevertheless, we fail to understand that fear also has power. People from all walks of life; deal with fear at some point in their lives. However, even though fear seems to be a common and a natural feeling, the Bible tells us, "Have I not commanded you? Be strong and courageous. Do not be afraid; do not be discouraged, for the LORD your God will be with you wherever you go." (Joshua 1:9). According to the Merriam-Webster's Learner's Dictionary, fear is defined as "an unpleasant, often strong emotion caused by anticipation or awareness of danger," and it adds that fear can be triggered by an "Anxious concern, reason for alarm and a profound reverence and awe especially toward God." From those notions of fears, the last one means reverence and honor to a higher being. In some cultures, fear can also be viewed as a sign of respect, because when children fear their parents, they tend to listen to their commands, and it is difficult to disobey or make the wrong choice.

Similarly, fear stems from a lack of knowledge and uncertainty of what is to come or not having control over circumstances. Dr. Michael Youssef (2015) described fear as "a normal and natural response to uncertain circumstances, but when we get to the point of living in a constant state of fear, we demonstrate a lack of trust in the One in whom we place our faith" (p. 5). "As real as fear may be, when we meditate day and night in God's Word, we prosper in all that we do" (Raley, D. & J., 2013). One immediate effect of fear is to demoralize and to shake our foundations. Fear blinds us from what is real and honest. Fear can paralyze every aspect of one's life and destroy dreams and aspirations. Many of us fail to reach our destination because we allow fear to take over and deprive us from our inheritance. Time and time again, when we do not lose sight of our goal, we can recall those powerful Words, "So do not fear, for I am with you; do not be dismayed, for I am your God. I will strengthen you and help you; I will uphold you with my righteous right hand" (Isaiah 41:10). Fear may be the dominant hindrance in your life. Fear may seem to be the driving force of your relationship, your career, and the bridge to your destiny, but remember there are ways to eliminate its authority over your life. Regardless how we have experienced fear, one thing we ought to know, it should not take over or rule over our lives.

2. Identify the Triggers of Fear

To the fearful person, life is unbearable, and every day presents various reasons or occasions to be afraid of some things or someone. Isn't it the life that we are living now? It can be a natural disaster, or something created by man. Understanding the cause of fear and the reason for the fear can prove to be a great way to manage it. "Triggers are any events or situations that cause a reaction; positive or negative" (dictionary.com). Fear is an emotional response to an event or some situations. It means some way or another anyone of us will face or encounter fear in the eye. Our reactions will determine the outcome.

Emotions are expressed in different forms. Being angry, frustrated, being happy, or being sad, crying after hearing some bad news or rejoicing are all type of emotions that all of us encounter daily. We cannot afford to say that one of those emotions are good and the other ones are bad; because it conveys how one is feeling mentally and it is a reaction for what occurs in a unique moment. The problem begins when fear gets out of control and impedes progress and success of a person. Once fear is recognized and identified, then you can use the lessons learned from that experience in other areas of your life and start making a difference. What may trigger fear in one person may not do so in another. Hence,

3

understanding the trigger is essential for the person affected. Once identified, the trigger is disabled, and the fear is resolved. "Do not be afraid of those who kill the body but cannot kill the soul. Rather, be afraid of the One who can destroy both soul and body in hell" (Matthew 10:28).

The act of being afraid can only take away from a person's ability to handle simple tasks. There is nothing good about fear. It devastates and renders its subject unproductive and unable to successfully live life to the fullest. As reported by Dr. Schaub (2009), "There is a saying in Alcoholics Anonymous that FEAR stand for False Evidence Appearing Real. The fact is most of our fear has no real danger, no real threat, connected to them" (p. 28). Therefore, as we can identify our fear, we are more likely to identify its source and uproot its branches of deception.

3. The Elements of Fear

Fear often begins with a lack of faith and an inability to discern reality from myths. Failures in general cause fear due to the expectations of one's self or other people's expectations. No one wants to disappoint loved ones. Failures cause embarrassment and possible disapproval. Failure also exposes doubt. The process of moving from failure or disapproval to success can be a daunting task that few are ready to undertake, but it is necessary nonetheless. Life's experiences will teach us quite often that failures are great opportunities to refocus and to access unknown tools that one would never use or discover if one had never failed. Failures are unique ways to reconnect and face unfavorable challenges of life. Failures are not the means to an end, but they are rather a time to stop, think, and reassess the situations so that mistakes can be repaired, and new methods can be utilized. "We are hard-pressed on every side, yet not crushed, we are perplexed, but not in despair;

4

persecuted, but not forsaken; struck down, but not destroyed" (2 Corinthians 4:8-9).

Failures are hard lessons learned that enable us to remember that life is not just only a gift, but it is a precious jewel that should not be taken for granted. Author, poet, and playwright Victor Hugo once stated, *"Those who live are those who fight."* Unfortunately, most of us, due to our thinking about what others may say about us, prefer to hide and lost opportunity that is entrenched in preparation. At times, we even allow people to cause us to flee far from the area where we failed out of shame and doubt. Let us imagine what would happen if a baby, after spending months of crawling on the floor, decided to stand up one day but failed on his many attempts because his family saw him stumble. Would that be the end of this journey for that baby? This alone is a great example for all of us to realize that certain things in life require many more attempts than others. However, we have been born with the natural will, will to succeed, will to accomplish our full potentials, and will to be affluent and defeat. Thich Nhat Hanh (2013), believed that *"we all experience fear, but if we can look deeply into our fear, we will be able to free ourselves, from its grip and touch joy"* (p. 6).

At times the enemy is playing games, so we do not reach our full potential and let fear dominate in our lives. If you only knew that you have wings, and those wings were for you to start flying, never will you continue to crawl. According to the Word of God, "... the Lord will make you the head and not the tail; you shall be above only, and not being beneath, if you heed the commandments of the Lord your God, which I command you today, and are careful to observe them" (Deuteronomy 28:13).

Those elements of fears cannot and should not hinder any of us to fulfill the potentials given to us, but also the reality of our destiny and will of God in our lives.

4. Struggles with Fear

Women and men unrelatedly of their ethnic or social background in general struggle with the idea of being accepted. Fear of rejection and not measuring up to the standards set by others can be a terrifying experience. "In short (or long) years of married life, I have struggled off and on with a fear of not measuring up to the ideal wife" (Newbell, 87).

As Christians, our role model is Jesus Christ. Therefore, we can seek approval from the Word of God, not the world. Usually, it is the other way around. For years, Christian women looked up to the Proverbs 31 woman that most of us are familiar with: "She is precious and giving." It is impossible for any woman to measure up to that woman. In fact, she does things such as sewing and cooking, and many women cannot perform these tasks. In Proverbs 31, the description of this ideal woman goes on to call her "blessed." "She is a business savvy and sews clothing…Who does both? Apparently, she does" (Newbell, 87). We can always be the best of ourselves, never by comparing ourselves to others. God's seed is in us, He has created us with special gifts and favor, but we let fear of the world and its false belief take over our lives. We will never be good enough in the eye of others, we will always have something that is not perfect, but we can always walk toward that perfection who is Jesus Christ. Wanting to talk like Him and be like Him is not an easy task but He will give us the strength and he will never reject us.

Understanding the root of fear is a great way to manage it and get rid of it. Newbell explains how the love of God, once understood, will be the ultimate safe haven in all situations. She uses 1 John 4:18-19, which states, "There is no fear in love, but perfect love casts out fear" (Newbell, p. 118). This type of fear referenced in the Bible is one of reverence and trust, not punishment and terror. Once we identify the reason behind the fear, we can begin to seek counsel and find ways to handle it. Zig Ziglar stated, "*Failure is a detour, not a dead-end street.*"

Fear can only be explained in the context of cause and effect. If we do not know the cause of our fears, we will not be able to conquer them, no matter how big our faith may be. Certain fears are caused by lack of information; someone who is afraid of water will probably not be afraid to be in a body of water where his or her feet touch the bottom. Because the feet are securely planted on the solid ground while in the water, the fear of drowning may dissipate at once, or when this person learn how to swim. On the other hand, fear of mutilation could have no basis and could be from a prior emotional or psychological event. Fear is a four-letter Word that can haunt someone's life if not grounded by the spirit. Fear is real. Even our Savior Jesus Christ, when it was time for Him to lay His life on the cross for our sins, He struggled to what's to come. However, he had the knowledge to go back to the Word and stated "Father, if you are willing, take this cup from me; yet not my will, but yours be done" (Luke 22: 42). Some way or another, we will be faced with fear and the struggles that it bears, but our way of dealing with it make the total transformation. Fear is a lie that you fed for so long that it wants to dominate over you. Fear hinders anyone to be set free. Fear is a mirage that creates uncertainty and false hope. Negative fear can impede anyone's ability to see the light and fulfill their full destiny. Polish-French chemist and physicist Marie Curie once stated, "*Nothing in life is to be feared, it is only to be understood.*"

CHAPTER II
B. PSYCHOLOGICAL AND EMOTIONAL SYMPTOMS OF FEAR

1. Paranoia and Doubt

The term paranoia comes from a Greek Word that means "madness." The term was used to describe a mental illness in which a delusional belief is the sole or prominent feature. The Diagnostic and Statistical Manual of Mental Disorders, Fifth Edition (DSM 5) explains that "paranoia involves intense anxious or fearful feelings and thoughts often related to persecution, threat, or conspiracy. Paranoia occurs in mental disorders; it becomes illusions in the presence of irrational thoughts" (mental health america.net). Although it is subjective, the emotion is real. This mental illness is diagnosed as criteria 301 on the DSM 5. The person affected by paranoia needs psychiatric help and needs to be taken seriously. It is easy to dismiss the person affected by paranoia as being "paranoid" with a tone of voice and attitude of disgust or lack of care. With compassion and respect, the person affected by paranoia can find needed help and may be able to rejoin society and live a productive life. Unfortunately, in certain cultures, paranoia is considered taboo. The person affected is treated as "crazy" and tends to be left on their own despair while the person needs mental help. The way the person is treated causes some people to abuse the person emotionally and at times physically.

The abuse received causes the person affected by paranoia to become doubtful about him or herself and withdraw from the society, and the isolation created often leads to depression. Depression can be clinical or nonclinical. If not dealt with, the doubt and increased anxiety can lead to more complications such as physical and psychological illnesses. The chain reaction can lead to more damage to the person's psyche or body.

We must point out depression is a state in people's life where their ways of thinking and acting can be detrimental to them and their surroundings. The lack of desire to enjoy what life has to offer or to have positive thoughts and being optimistic is nonexistent. More often, people lose interest in the things that used to bring joy to their lives when they are going through the state of depression. Every so often the mood changes also affect sleep, habits, and ways of functioning. Depression has no mercy on anyone, regardless of your profession, or social financial status. However, it is treatable when one seeks assistance and gets the necessary support. This physical and emotional feeling of hopelessness is not of God, yet, we have seen many powerful leaders in the Bible struggling with the feeling of bleakness. Hence, focusing and remaining in the Word of God ought to be a constant source. "Worry weighs a person down, and encouraging Word cheers a person up." (Proverbs 12: 25).

Christians ought to understand and remember the scriptures. We have been given the most powerful antidote, medicine and natural treatment that can only come from the Word of God; The Bible "For God is not the author of confusion but of peace, as in all the churches of the saints" (1 Corinthians 14:33). God cannot afford to lead us to the wrong path because He is the path, the light, and His Word is Him. Luke 11:13 reminded us that God is an amazing father. "If you then, being evil, know how to give good gifts to your children, how much more will your heavenly Father give the Holy Spirit to those who ask Him?"

According to experts, paranoia is often time the result of over thinking and analyzing fear. However, according to the Bible, faith serves as the antidote that casts all fears and it manifests itself on a multidimensional level.

2. Sleep Disorders

Many of us are often sleep deprived because we are concerned about things that we do not have any control over. Yet, we think by losing sleep over it; maybe things will be better. Unfortunately, things do not just getter better. Sleep disorders involve problems with the quality, timing, and amount of sleep, which cause problems with functioning and distress during the daytime (www.psychiatry.org).

It is unfortunate that some of us are unable to enjoy a great night of sleep due to work or some troubling events or challenges that we are facing daily. Yes, those challenges are real and seem at times unbearable. Our body was made to not only make movement, however, the resting of our thoughts and physical body can benefit one equally. If not having enough sleep can trigger someone's ability to perform daily living activity. Consequently, fear causes anxiety, which in turn keeps the body in a fight-or-flight state. This maintains the body's circulation at a level where the person is very alert and active, and in that state of mind, the fearful person is unable to relax enough to fall asleep. Sleep disorders can damage the body in the long run. For this reason, the Bible teaches us that there is a time for everything, "To everything there is a season, a time for every purpose under heaven" (Ecclesiastes 3:1).

Sleep is needed for the body to reproduce cells and tissue. Imagine the person with a sleep disorder having to work full-time. Several problems can occur at the workplace with lack of sleep and decreased alertness. The person becomes inefficient and could end up being a liability for the company and the people he or she works with. There are several types of sleep disorders of which "Insomnia is the most common" (www.psychiatric.org). In the primary care, 10-20 percent of people complain of significant sleep problems, which represents a 30 percent increase from 1999 to 2010. Did you know the number of prescriptions for sleep medications increased approximately by 200 percent in the same period? This evidence sheds light on the magnitude of sleep disorders and its implications for those affected.

Many patients took medication to fall asleep, but their pains and fear are stronger than the medicine and still were unable to fall asleep. A lack of sleep means a lack of focus, concentration, and ability to relax. We become unstable, and we cannot connect to the beauty and a peaceful mind. Sometimes, this is where we need to be wise and remember what it says in the serenity prayer. "God, grant me the serenity to accept the things I cannot change, courage to change the things I can, and wisdom to know the difference" (Reinhold Niebuhr, 1943). We are not armed to do everything on our own we need to remember that we are not alone.

3. Mental Regression

In a psychological context, going back to early or past behavior is termed "regression". Originally, Sigmund Freud classified regression as "a defense mechanism for coping with stress; where one reverts to earlier, more childlike patterns of behavior to cope" (Sisgold, 2011). Because regression usually has to do with stress and anxiety, the level of regression can be linked to where we are, physically, emotionally and spiritually in our journey. As well as the knowledge of whom we are in Christ. Hence, it is important that we know what we are worth and take advantage of where we are in our lives to make the best out of it; so many of us are walking backward in our journey to life in regression mode. The things of the past became our weakest skill whereas we should have been matured enough to handle them.

We encounter people who wish to be or wish to have but are unable to make sense of their own reality. We have learned if we are happy with what we have, what we have will make us happy. Unfortunately, we are blindsided by what we wish for, while today is up for grab and we let it go by. Many of us live in the "if world" while the present is escaping away from us. Countless of us were to be in a state of changing lives, making an impact in the lives of our neighbor until now we cannot sustain on our own. "You have been believers so long now that you ought to be teaching others. Instead, you need someone to teach you again the basic things about God's Word. You are like babies who need milk and cannot eat solid food" (Hebrew 5:12).

Debbie McDaniel one of the iBelieve contributors shared on one of her blogs *Find hope in the Storm* "Fear is one of the enemy's favorite weapons". Worry, anxiety, fear, can overwhelm all of us like a thick shadow of darkness, controlling our every move and decision. Yet reality tells us that so much of what we spend our time worrying about never even happens. Living under the weight of the "what if's" is a hard place to dwell. How many of us are still in that mental regression and hidden from the sun of truth in our daily lives. It is time for us to wake up from that dream that seems to be a reality but so disengaged with the promises and the word of God upon us. "Fear not, for I am with you; be not dismayed, for I am your God; I will strengthen you, I will help you, I will uphold you with my righteous right hand". Psalms 34: 4.

Fear will always be in our lives, therefore how we engage or disengaged when it surfaces in our lives can be the factor in ways it can damage our relationship and our ways of living life.

CHAPTER III
C. UNHEALTHY FEAR

There are many types of fear that may require treatment because if not treated they may lead to death. We have the power to change the statistics when we take the time to listen and to observe what is going on around us. Among all these fears are the fear of the unknown, natural disasters, being alone, financial instability, disease, ISIS and death. Some of these fears are not only real, but we cannot escape from them. Hence, our behavior and ability to navigate during those fearful times generate character.

1. Fear of the Unknown

None of us are privileged to know what tomorrow may hold. However, most of us spend time stressing about situations that we do not have any control over. "Many are the plans in a person's heart, but it is the Lord's purpose that prevails" (Proverbs 19:21). If we can grasp the idea that we do not have control over a lot of things in our lives and that our destiny relies on God's hand, we will worry less about the unknown. "Do not be anxious about anything, but in every situation, by prayer and petition, with thanksgiving, present your requests to God. And the peace of God, which transcends all understanding, will guard your hearts and your minds in Christ Jesus" (Philippians 4:6-7). "Living in constant fear affects our relationships, warps our view of reality, and distorts our view of God" (Dr. Youssef, 2015. p. 6).

During a documentary about white sharks in 2014, one of the divers defended the white shark, as he was talking about their behaviors and how people misunderstood their activities in the water. He stated that, the fear of the white shark may prompt us to respect the unknown. As opposed to fear the white sharks and the unknown, let us respect what we don't

13

know. This was a powerful statement because we are more likely to judge and let fear dominate that which we are having trouble understanding. If we can only pause for a quick moment. We will realize sometimes it is not about understanding of what is different; it is the desire to learn and to accept difference that should be our focus. In the book, *Devotions for Every Day of the Year: Jesus Calling*, Young (2004) indicated, your own "understanding will never bring you Peace…God's instruction is to trust Him, not in your understanding" (p. 230).

3. Fear of Natural Disasters

Flood, hurricane, landslides, tornadoes, volcanic eruptions, mudslide, or earthquakes are natural disasters that surpass mankind power and intelligence. Scientists, researchers and the most gifted cannot stop or manage how much damage those natural disasters are able to do in a state or a country. The earthquakes of 2010 in Haiti, China, Chile, Indonesia, and Turkey taught us as a people and as nations that we do not have and will never have control over all things. Those nations felt lost and dumbfounded. They did not know where to go from that point. With so many lost lives and disruption in everyday lives, government leaders from all over the world had the urge to step up and assist a nation in need. What to do and how to help the country rebuild were key questions that had to be answered fast. However, the fear and the lives of those people were forever changed by something that they had no control or power over. Subsequently, what do you do? What do you do in front of the inevitable?

Fear of the unknown kept many in bondage and as one nation was trying to search and save those under debris, the people in Chile, China were also in disbelief because once again, another earth quake claims the lives of many families.

Parents looking for their children, and children looking for their parents, created an added confusion and total chaos. This type of fear disables the mind and the body to the point of mental instability. Years after the earthquakes, the need for rebuilding and restoring life to its previous status remains a challenge that many leaders meet with great trepidation. Reality is no longer tangible.

Generally, fear is disabling to the body and the mind, but on a national or international scale, fear of the unknown can present serious complications for those who must actively rise to the occasion. How do you upsurge to an occasion you have never experienced? How do you rise to a situation that is far stronger than you and beyond your abilities? Even though it is reported that 2017 was the third warmest year on record, according to the National Oceanic and Atmospheric Administration (NOAA), in the United States of America, there were 16 natural disasters in 2017 that caused more than $1 billion in damage each. Hurricanes caused a total of $265 billion in damage, including $125 billion from Hurricane Harvey, $90 billion for Hurricane Maria and $50 billion from Hurricane Irma.

Natural disaster teaches us that intelligence or money is just a tool that human kind seeks, but there is a greater being that has control over all things. What we need is wisdom and how to adjust when disaster strikes. Natural disaster may be beyond our control; but the ability to live and get back up again is a powerful skill. Learning to surrender may be our greatest asset in understanding how important and how fragile life remains. Now it is evident that no one is justified before God by the law, for "The righteous shall live by faith" (Galatians 3:11).

4. Fear of Being Alone

There have been many stories about married people who agree to stay in an emotionally and physically abusive relationship because they are afraid of being alone. Too many spouses have lost their lives with the hope of they can help or change an abusive partner. Marriage is one of the most difficult yet most rewarding blessings when two souls agreed to live life faithfully.

Believers have to hold on to the Word of God: "Though my father and mother forsake me, the LORD will receive me (Psalm 27:10). Furthermore, God did not create us to be living in suffering and be mistreated by our spouses. On the contrary, His Word said, "Husbands, love your wives, just as Christ also loved the church and gave Himself for her to make her holy" (Ephesians 5:25. Because the fear of being alone is layered with so many past experiences from parents and past relationships, as well as concerns of how society will judge or see them, some people lose sight of who they are to project a false image of what God has intended them to live not in fear and despair but to live free. Apostle Paul added, "Cleansing her by the washing with water through the Word, and to present her to himself as a radiant church, without stain or wrinkle or any other blemish, but holy and blameless (Ephesians 5:26-27). Many of us come to this world as twins or triplets, and a small number of us are born as quadruplets, quintuplets, sextuplets, septuplets and even nonuplets. However, most us come to this world alone, and God in His faithfulness guides our paths and made us fulfilled. Therefore, we are never alone. "And surely, I am with you always, to the very end of the age" (Matthew 28:20).

Loneliness bring sadness and desperation nevertheless, sometimes being alone can be the healthiest way to be happy again.

CHAPTER IV
D. THE GREAT RECESSION AND OTHER FEARS

1. The Great Recession

The great recession of 2008 was one of the worst financial crises in the history of the United States. Many lost their minds, their homes, and their families due to financial hardship. The world seemed to be going backwards and could not believe that all that was happening in the markets was real. For many, it was a bad dream that they wrestled with. When money is the most valuable entity in your life, you are missing out all the great gifts that you are surrounded with. The people of God need to be reminded of God's grace and mercy and not be fearful about what the world is saying.

The world keeps on changing and there is always something good or something not so good coming our way. As much we believe that we know better and that we can prevent certain situations from happening; unfortunately, we will never be able to avoid the unavoidable. Hereafter, our reaction and humility toward what is and what is to come should be our mantra. In the United States alone, hunger is manifested daily, and it is screaming in many cities and towns. However, food, clothing, the basic living things are wasted daily. Consequently, recession may help people readjust their lives in making better decision in their habits, daily spending and focus on what truly matters. Talking about management and rationalization may seem foreign for many when it was never being a topic of discussion in many families.

From past recession, people around the world tend to react as opposed to learn from the past. There are many countries around the world where poverty seems to be the word of the day or the norm. Yet, those people remain with a joy and 'joie de vivre' that is beyond understanding. God can and will provide our needs, regardless of what the economy says. "So, He humbled you, allowed you to hunger, and fed you with manna which you did not know nor did your fathers know, that He might make you know that man shall not live by bread alone; but man lives by every Word that proceeds from the mouth of the Lord" (Deuteronomy 8:3). When all seems out of control, believers should believe that we do not live by sight but by faith. "And my God shall supply all your need according to His riches in glory by Christ Jesus (Philippians 4:19).

2. Fear of Financial Instability

In 2010 the stock market took a tumble that made everyone realize that money is certainly not what makes life worth living. However, some people rely on their bank account and sacrifice their whole life working, without realizing that the true meaning of life resides in true relationships with one another. Regardless of the relationship one may have with one another or even money, this association needs to be a healthy one. To have a healthy relationship it requires hard work and hard work demands discipline and some understanding. Fear of financial instability is one of the most stressful fear because it requires one to live in a constant survival mode and worrying about the uncontrollable. It happens too often that financial fear lead many to live a life of charlatan, lies, and controversies to maintain a certain standard and appearance. We all know too well how appearance can be such a deceiving act and more temptation and obsession for success. In November 2008, the world discovered how Bernie Madoff pulled off the biggest Ponzi scheme in history by ripping a size of $64.8 billion to his 4,800 clients. At times one may not have money but having charity, a conscience is worth more than billions. It is said too often that *giving is typically better than receiving.* Hence, fear of financial instability can lead to a greater debt.

18

During his passage on the earth, Jesus Christ was tested on the wilderness after fasting for forty days and forty nights. In his moment of need the tempter came to Him by telling him to turn the stones into bread to satisfy his hunger. As opposed to let hunger and temptation take over, He responded to the devil… "It is written: 'Man shall not live on bread alone, but on every word, that comes from the mouth of God". Matthew 4: 4. Yes, the reality of life and the demands pushed us to live in fear as opposed to live a productive life of giving, honor and compassion. We tend to forget what matter most in life is not only the pursuit of money but a well-balanced life. It is also noted in one of the Bible's stories how a certain woman after the passing of her husband that her creditor did not show any compassion or charity but having his money back was his priority, or this lady's two sons will turn into slaves. Because she was a servant who feared the LORD; not the financial crisis, she finds favor from the prophet named Elisha who helped her exercise her faith in the symbol of oil to pay her debt.

Money when not managed properly can bring a sense of instability and fear. Yet, the comfort and the flexibility it offers is also important to recognize. Peter Ruberton, a doctoral candidate in social-personality psychology at the University of California, Riverside, who was the lead author of a study on how your bank account affects your mood, reported, "No matter how much the customers had or earned, no matter how much debt they had, having a buffer of easily accessible cash was associated with greater happiness." If the world depends on their bank accounts to find joy or happiness, we believers must depend on God because the earth is the Lord's, as well as everything in it, the world, and all who live in it; for he founded it on the seas and established it on the waters" (Psalm 24:1–2). We encounter many people in different cultures who don't depend on their bank accounts to survive and maintain a life of peace and honor; when the fear of financial instability can be a burden for many. There are greater gifts that can take precedence over our lives that can give us a sense of accomplishment. Galatians 5: 22-23 "But the fruit of the Spirit is love, joy, peace, forbearance, kindness, goodness, faithfulness, gentleness and self-control. Against such things there is no law".

3. Fear of Diseases, Zika Virus, and ISIS

In the early 1980s, four groups were labeled as having the predisposition towards the disease HIV/AIDS. They were called "4-H": hemophiliacs, heroin addicts, homosexuals, and Haitians. At that time, people feared each of these unique populations. The members of these groups had to find unique ways to continue to exist notwithstanding that stigma. While researchers tried to develop some type of treatment for AIDS, it is still slowly killing people from all walks of life. As we fast-forward thirty years, new fears continue to shake the world: cancer, Zika virus, and ISIS. Christians need to understand that "what has been, will be again; what has been done will be done again; there is nothing new under the sun" (Ecclesiastes 1:9).

Viruses do not have a cure. However, researchers have come up with ways of managing the symptoms. The first case of the Zika virus was uncovered in 2008, but not many people heard much about it. According to the Centers for Disease Control and Prevention (2016), it is reported that Zika is a disease caused by Zika virus that is spread to people primarily through the bite of an infected mosquito (Aedes aegypti and Aedes albopictus). The most common symptoms of Zika are fever, rash, joint pain, and conjunctivitis (red eyes). Pregnant women may be at more risk because of the effects on the unborn baby (namely microcephaly, which is a very small, deformed head). One thing people should know is that Zika is not a new virus. In May 2015, the Pan American Health Organization (PAHO) issued an alert regarding the first confirmed Zika virus infection in Brazil. Since that time, additional transmissions have been reported at other territories and countries. Hence, here is a disease that people are afraid of because they are now aware of it. What has been called news on television or any form of media has been promoted by an atmosphere of fear, desolation, and despair.

About five thousand people died in the U.S. on September 11, 2011. Since then, a new era of fear has been demoralizing people around the world, the Islamic State in Iraq and Syria. Just because of the idea that ISIS exists, some people can no longer sleep, travel, or have a normal life. Most of us have been living on the edge. If it is not ISIS, it is a random shooting that claims the lives of bystanders or crimes on the disfranchised neighborhoods. This is where and when we, believers, should always be connected and aware of what the Word of God says: "A thousand may fall at your side, ten thousand at your right hand, but it will not come near you" (Psalm 91:7). Furthermore, if God allows for something to happen, remember that "the righteous person may have many troubles, but the LORD delivers him from them all; he protects all his bones, not one of them will be broken" (Psalm 34:19-20)

4. Fear of Death and Dying

Most of us tend to rejoice when a new baby is born. However, whenever a person passes away, most of us have a hard time dealing with the pain and emotional toll that the loss brings into our lives. It helps to recognize ourselves as part of a great cycle and find comfort in the fact that everyone else must go through the same cycles: conception, birth, and death. Remembering those we loved and cherished is also a normal process. "For to me; to live is Christ and to die is gain" (Philippians 1:21). For Christians, death should be embraced

21

and be a reminder of God's promise to us. He will never forsake us, and even in our death, we are not alone. It is important for us to come to terms with the fact that death is unavoidable. We should be in a place to grasp the idea of life's balance. Our perception and where we stand when tough times come can be the very difference in our lives.

In her book, *Death and Dying*, Elisabeth Kübler-Ross (1997) outlined the five stages that dying patient's experience, which are denial, anger, bargaining, depression, and acceptance. While a patient is dealing with those stages, family members are also trying to make amends with a reality that seems a mirage, and they take the time to get to the point of accepting and saying goodbye. Martin Luther King Jr stated, "The ultimate measure of a man is not where he stands in moments of comfort and convenience, but where he stands at times of challenge and controversy."

Believers' definition of death ought to have a different meaning than just pain and desolation. "Let the dead bury their own dead, but you go and proclaim the kingdom of God" (Luke 9:60). We have a responsibility to not dwell on those who have transitioned ahead of us because we have hope that we will see them again. Because of that insurance alone, we should be comforted. This example is a reminder that we need to understand that it is vital that we take the time to appreciate the people around us, the special gift called life and to be prepared always.

Death is a natural passage for all of us. "For we must all appear before the judgment seat of Christ, so that each of us may receive what is due us for the things done while in the body, whether good or bad." (2 Corinthians 5:10). If we want to be a follower of Jesus (disciple or student), to look like him and to do the things that He has done; we cannot pick and choose which episode of His life we want to live and what part of it we want to exclude. "I am He who lives, and was dead, and behold, I am alive forevermore. Amen. And I have the keys of Hades and of Death" (Revelation 1:18).

Fear has more power in our daily lives than we want to admit. Therefore, regardless of what hinders you from reaching your full potential fear of the unknown, fear of natural disasters, fear of being alone, or anything in your life that you are trying to overcome. It is imperative to step back and to remind yourself that everything starts with your own perception and your own attitude. In *Mindset, the New Psychology of Success*, Dweck (2006) shared how our behaviors and our coping strategies depend on our mind-set. As believers, where do we stand when the world is bombarded with fear? What keeps us moving along? What is our mind-set when the challenges in life seem inevitable? Fear can be the negative energy that hinders you from reaching your full potential. Fear can have so much power over your life that it can handicap you from the great things that God has in store for you.

Now that you have a better sense of what fear can do to you, how do you decide to prevail and stand as a conqueror? This next section will help you decide and analyze who you are, whom you belong to, and how it is time to deprogram and unravel the mystery of fear and to claim your victory, your purpose, your goal, and your deliverance from dream to reality.

Do not be a skeptic; it is the trick of the enemy. Let's embark to a new frontier of optimism where you can move from the bondage of lies, the illusion of fear, the feeling of being unworthy. Empower yourself to reach that next level of authority, your full potential, the next phase, the dimension to unleash the power, the peace, the anointing the favor and the true blessing that you are. Furthermore, Jesus reminded us on John 16: 33 "I have told you these things, so that in me you may have peace. In this world you will have trouble. But take heart! I have overcome the world."

CHAPTER V
E. DEPROGRAMMING; HEALTHY FEAR

Regardless of the situation that one faces, it is imperative for people to change their ways of thinking to address the situation with abilities and techniques. According to Dr. Caroline Leaf, "Change in your thinking is essential to detox the brain. Consciously controlling your thought life means not letting thoughts rampage…It means learning to engage interactively with every single thought" (drleaf.com). It is so much easier to sit back and allow negative thoughts to saturate our minds to the point of dysfunction. While it is easy to learn new information to better ourselves, it is very difficult to unlearn destructive thought patterns that can too often destroy our lives and others' in our circle. Dr. Leaf explains how our own thoughts can wreak havoc in our lives and render us ineffective and even disable to some extent. She found that "75 to 95 percent of the illnesses that plague us today are a direct result of our thought life" (drleaf.com).

If our thought process has that much impact on our daily lives, then we must consider ways and means of deprogramming and reprogramming the process so that we may be able to live better and productive lives. This research provides us with ample tools so that we can be better and stronger people. Therefore, we may, in turn, create and maintain great relationships that glorify God and build stronger families. Thus, the relationship between fear and faith can be aided by knowledge of how to recognize and identify the need to deprogram and reprogram so that healing can take place.

Deprogramming and reprogramming can very much be overwhelming, as anything learned is committed to memory. How does one tell the mind to unlearn something? "By looking at the thought process" (drleaf.com), Reversing the thought process is not as easy as one might think.

It takes time, energy, and a willingness to let go of previous information so that new information may be learned and utilized. The process of deprogramming can be painful and uncomfortable. For example, a woman who has been abused by her husband learns to be afraid of men in general and all authority figures. To unlearn that type of fear, she must decide to overcome the fear and open herself up to learning new skills, so she can move on with her life. There is no set time for the deprogramming and reprogramming process. Once the process begins, it could take months or years, but essentially the end goal is to be healed and become whole. From dysfunction to being functional in all aspects of life is the goal. Believers need to be in a stage in their lives wherein they are led by the spirit of the Lord. For us to conquer anything it must be a total surrender. We are unable to reach our full potential and what we can do because our strength does not come from us but from God alone. The Apostle Paul said it well, "I have been crucified with Christ; it is no longer I who live, but Christ lives in me; and the life which I now live in the flesh I live by faith in the Son of God, who loved me and gave Himself for me" (Galatians 2:20).

To understand fear in relation to faith takes knowledge, wisdom, and the courage to step out of one's comfort zone. Where there is love, there is also courage and the strength to give unselfishly. Faith in love gives the courage to tackle any task. Once faith is established, then fear has no power over the mind. For those of us who know the Lord, His Word, and His will for our lives, we can easily apply this verse, but for the non-Christians, their fear is often rooted in a lack of knowledge of God. Fear comes easy and invades our lives, but to get rid of it may take years. Our problem with fear and faith almost always has to do with our need for approval and appreciation.

1. Fear of the Lord

When we take the time to contemplate on nature and to realize the structure of the sun, the moon, the sea, human being and everything around; one must admit there is a greater power who took time to organize and assemble all these wonders in perfect harmony. The best way to know and to stay connected to God is through a total surrender and reverence to whom He is and where wisdom comes from. "Holy fear is the key to God's sure foundation, unlocking the treasuries of salvation, wisdom, and knowledge" (Bevere, 2006).

As some of us look at the universe and understand that it is all about science, believers contemplate the glory and the vastness of the universe as the work of the Most High. The simplest feeling of reverence and respect overwhelmingly touches our hearts and souls upon acknowledging the majesty and glory of God. "But God made the earth by his power. He founded the world by his wisdom and stretched out the heavens by his understanding. When He thunders, the waters in the heavens roar; He makes clouds rise from the ends of the earth. He sends lightning with the rain and brings out the wind from His storehouses" (Jeremiah 10:12-13).

Fear of the Lord is the healthiest fear of all because of the peace, the wisdom, and the total surrender of obedience and comfort that it grooms in our hearts and in our minds. We are dealing with someone who sees us as sons and daughters. "As a father has compassion on his children, so the Lord has compassion on those who fear him; for he knows how we are formed, he remembers that we are dust" (Psalm103:13–14). Furthermore, as Newbell reported, "To fear the Lord is not to be scared of Him. It's to adore Him. Worship Him. Honor Him; it is to put Him in the right place in our thinking" (p. 119).

2. Fear to Live in Sin

It is not always easy to do the right thing because it requires much effort, resistance and a strong will. Hence, living a life of lies, appearance and feeling good tend to be tempting at times. Because we have been created in Christ's image and we can inherit some qualities that can only come from the Lord, we are unable to live a life of sins daily. We will make mistakes, we will fall and tumble at times, and however, a true believer does not live a life of sins purposely. "For we are God's handiwork, created in Christ Jesus to do good works, which God prepared in advance for us to do" (Ephesians 2:10). When our relationship with God is the pivotal point in our lives, and it matters so much; we must do our best even though it will cost us friendships, relationships, jobs or opportunities.

We have been called to live a purposeful life that is originated according to God's Word, will, and way. Sometimes we have an obligation to flee from wrongdoing because our relationship with God matters much more than a minute of sin. As the say goes, *think twice, act/speak once*. In the book of Matthew 11:12 it is reported ... "until now the kingdom of heaven suffers violence, and the violent take it by force". How much are we ready to give up reaching the greatest prize? Think of some challenges in your life as a battle, not the war. Each little combat, every temptation you confronted can only make you the best that you have called to be. Joseph flee from Potiphar's wife. Refusing to go to bed with her. (Genesis 39).

Don't sell yourself short. There is so much more in you than fit the eyes. When you encounter the next attraction, the feeling-good moment, remember it is temporary and there are so many desirable moments waiting at the end. "Therefore, submit to God. Resist the devil and he will flee from you." As a human, we will make mistakes, but we cannot stay and live in sin.

Sins ought to be an accident in the life of a believer, not a habit or way of living. Never forget that we are saved because of Jesus' sacrifice and not because of our good deeds. "For it is by grace you have been saved, through faith and this is not from yourselves, it is the gift of God not by works, so that no one can boast" (Ephesians 2:8 - 9). Many of us chose a life of sins because it is not easy to follow rules and expectations set for us. Others chose to do whatever they feel like doing because they are driven by their feelings. Feelings are not always constant; it varies from a moment to another. It is not always easy to do the right thing and to live life free of sins. However, deciding to live a righteous life can only be granted when we are willing to be set apart. Set a part sometimes means a life of solitude and discomfort. Doing the right thing requires sacrifices and saying resounding **no** to our own desires and yes to God's word. Overall, regardless of our backgrounds, all of us deal with a level of fear in some way or another. Fear is one thing that seems universal. Most of the believers are comforted by the provisions, the salvation, and the intimate relationship they have with God. In 1 John1: 7 it states, "But if we walk in the light, as he is in the light, we have fellowship with one another, and the blood of Jesus, his Son, purifies us from all sin".

Fear dominates the first section of this book because it is real, and some people must reach that level of understanding, deprogramming their minds to be in the mindset of confidence to reach and discover their real purpose. Therefore, let us unleash the armor of faith to battle the attack of the enemy. We know that his plan it to destroy us but by grace the victory is ours. Hence, let us stay connected to unravel the light the power of God that lives inside of us. We are unable to defeat the complications and trials faced with our own strength and eyes, "For our struggle is not against flesh and blood, but against the rulers, against the authorities, against the powers of this dark world and against the spiritual forces of evil in the heavenly realms (Ephesians 2:12).

3. Healthy Fear of Being Alone

There is a gross misunderstanding between loneliness and being alone. Those who suffer from loneliness deal with that feeling of constant and quotidian discontent. Being lonely is a negative and uncomfortable state that is empowered by a feeling of isolation; a sensation of loss and despair. It does not matter if you are sitting home alone or if you are in a big crowd and accompanied by friends and family members. That dull feeling is constant and is pulling you so hard that it is difficult to move away from it. The mere thought of being alone creates undue fears in some people. Insecurity, anxiety, and depression can often lead to a feeling of paranoia to the point where we are overwhelmed by the fear of being alone. The real problem comes when this type of fear causes us to be needy and hovering. Once the fear crosses all boundaries, such as not allowing other people to have adequate space to be them, treatment is necessary.

Being alone can be a healthy choice that does not involve any negative feelings. It could also mean a more comfortable place to be when needed. Some people take the time to better themselves to learn new skills, enhance their way of living or focus on what really matters to them. Others, after trials of being in some failed relationships and learning they are better friends than a companionship can also determine to be alone is the best choice. Deciding to be or to live alone without a partner can be the best option for anyone who chose that way of life. However, we are by nature prone to live with one another as well as being a helper to those around us. Genesis 2:18 revealed "The Lord God said, "It is not good for the man to be alone. I will make a helper suitable for him."

Barbara Streisand sings, "People who need people are the luckiest people in the Word" (Streisand, 1964). That song "People," was composed by Jule Styne with lyrics by Bob Merrill for the 1964 Broadway musical *Funny Girl* starring

Barbra Streisand. The simplicity, logic, and humility of that song remind us that to need others is an essential and normal sensation that makes us whole again. The Word of God teaches us, "So we, being many, are one body in Christ, and individually members of one another" (Romans 12:5). Being in a relationship with one another is beneficial because there is strength and power in numbers. "Two are better than one because they have a good reward for their labor" (Ecclesiastes 4: 9). We were created to support, to love, respect and to work with one another "Therefore, as we have the opportunity, let us do good to all, especially to those who are of the household of faith" (Galatians 6:10).

While there is a great difference between being alone in a relationship with a partner rather than a helper; not all of us are being called to a life of marital or intimate relationship with one another. Therefore, how does one know for sure when called for an intimate or marital life? Paul reminded us, "Sometimes I wish everyone were single like me a simpler life in many ways! But celibacy is not for everyone any more than marriage is. God gives the gift of the single life to some, the gift of the married life to others" (1 Corinthians 7:7). It seems evident that gift is something that should not be taken for granted. We cannot judge someone who has decided to live a life of celibacy or a marital life. Each one of them requires a certain skill, devotion and a special gift.

Unfortunately, we realized that we have been received that gift when faced with a situation. Until now, some of us are currently debating which way to go, and how do we know if we have the gift to be alone or in a relationship with someone. The response is within us. However, life situation or what society is requiring from us, unable us to reach the level of honesty and truth within ourselves. Regardless of the challenges one is facing, it is vital to seek an answer in prayer and in connection with the Lord. As we seek the Lord, one rather be in an intimate relationship with Him than look for anything else. Isn't it true that His presence is sweeter than honey, more expensive than gold? If His presence is sweeter than honey, He became our priority. When God has precedence over one life, everything else becomes less significant. "But seek first the kingdom of God and his righteousness, and all these things will be added to you" (Matthew 6: 33).

As we give God precedence over our lives, a mate, children and anything else will be secondary. We will appreciate them as oppose to make them our idolatry. The Book of Genesis in chapter 1: 28 reminded us when He created mankind said "Be fruitful and increase in number; fill the earth and subdue it. Rule over the fish in the sea and the birds in the sky and over every living creature that moves on the ground." Those revelations are not empty promises, they are chosen Words, beneficial for those who believe and put Him first. 1 Corinthians 7:32-33 says, "… I want you to be free from concern. One who is unmarried is concerned about the things of the Lord, how he may please the Lord; but one who is married is concerned about the things of the world, how he may please his wife".

One must know for sure pleasing God is more significant than pleasing the flesh or the world. So often, we miss out on life, lost fragile and important part of our destiny due to fear. A pregnancy terminated, stealing from others, idolatry, a life of lies, etc. A mistake will and can always be a mistake, just remember that we serve a God that love us unconditionally, regardless of our errors. He is willing to restore and to transform our lives during our slips ups if we ask for forgiveness. He won't judge us but will forgive and give us a new beginning. Unfortunately, forgiving ourselves, and accepting that God has forgiveness can be a challenge. It is only the work or the enemy; to make us doubt.

4. Fear is

Fear is an annoying habit that refuses to stop.
Fear is a thief that opens an unlocked door.
Fear is a gate to nowhere.
Fear is a disloyal friend who refuses to let you go.
Fear is a mirage of a house without an exit door.
Fear is the step that holds us back.
Fear is a handicap that hinders us from walking.
Fear is an obsessed fact that gives the same result.
Fear is a lie that you heard in a young age.
Fear is the nonchalance to get better.
Fear is giving up before the battle.
Fear is a ruthless enemy.
Fear is a blindfold cloth that is transparent.
Fear is walking as opposed to flying.
Fear is the helplessness to claim what's yours.
Fear is the shadow of a small rock far away.
Fear is the key to the wrong door.
Fear is wasted potentiality.
Fear is a gifted musician without his instrument.
Fear is a plane that never takes off.
Fear is an elevator without button that traps us.
Fear is negativity without a magnet of truth.
Fear is static.
Fear is a disloyal partner who pretends to be honest
Fear is everywhere.
Fear is venomous.
Fear is a lack of passion and will to live.
Fear is the opponent that you don't see.
Fear is darkness in a sunny day.

(Soraya P. Calixte, 2017)

CHAPTER VI
F. MOVING FROM FEAR TO FAITH

Faith cannot be grasped by a simple definition. It is that total conviction that is beyond intellectual belief or reasoning. Faith is not a visible object that you can test and prove if it exists or if you have it. Even though, all of us some way or another have witnessed and exercised faith, but we usually conclude faith in the aftermath of an event.

In the Christian life, faith becomes the pivotal force that leads and guides one's path: "For it is by grace you have been saved, through faith and this is not from yourselves, it is the gift of God not by works, so that no one can boast. For we are God's handiwork, created in Christ Jesus to do good works" (Ephesians 2:8-10) The Word of God is clearly defining for those who believe in the elements of faith and its relationship to grace. Therefore, understanding faith is only possible through an open communication with God as we learn about His will for our lives. "Consequently, faith comes by hearing, and hearing by the word of God" (Romans 10:17).

It became obvious that 'faith comes by hearing was noted for a reason. It meant, all of us have the same privilege, the equal ability and capacity to hear the Word. Accordingly, how we received what we hear can make an impact in the lives of those who believe. However, there is tremendous alteration between hearing and listening. According to the student Handbook of the University of Minnesota Duluth, it is noted: "Hearing is simply the act of perceiving sound by the ear" ... "Listening, however, is something you consciously choose to do. It means that listening requires concentration so that your brain processes meaning from words and sentences. Listening leads to learning". This notation is important because the Word of God requires the gift of the Holy Spirit and a close relationship with Him to grasp the real meaning and depth of this faith that is through grace.

33

We know that there is a close relationship between grace faith and our salvation. Thus, we must also understand what the Word of God says about the characterization of faith in relation to fear. It may seem that some people are excluded from experiencing faith. However, all of us are using faith to navigate our daily lives consciously or unconsciously. We make plans for tomorrow, as though we know for certain that we will be around. We sit down on a chair without thinking about whether it will withstand our weight or not. We drive a car because we believe it will bring us from a place to another, although sometimes it fails to bring us to our destination; yet we still rely on that car. We live life daily with the expectations that so many things will just follow their natural course. That expectation alone, can also be considered as faith in action! Therefore, we cannot afford to take our lives for granted and forgetting that a sacrifice was made, and a price was paid. God sent His only Son who die for us, so we can enjoy this life that has been given to us by grace for free.

We believe in the things that we create, but we forget that we have a creator, who is the source of all things. We fail to value and take authority of the unrestricted power that has been given to us. The Word of God has the power and the ability to transform thoughts and ideas and to cause us to live by faith. This form of transformation is essential to our everyday lives. "All Scripture is God-breathed and is useful for teaching, rebuking, correcting and training in righteousness, so that the servant of God may be thoroughly equipped for every good work" (2 Timothy 3:16 - 17).

We cannot make it without the Word. "For the Word of God is alive and active. Sharper than any double-edged sword, it penetrates even to dividing soul and spirit, joints and marrow; it judges the thoughts and attitudes of the heart" (Hebrews 6:12). If we want to please God, we ought to live according to His will, and His Word while reaching our goals successfully.

Many of us are not so sure about His will, many times we think this whole idea of faith and the Word of God is simply some type of conspiracy theory to make people slave, robotic and chained in their mind and evolution. As much we question ourselves about the world and our surrounding it is palpable truth there is something that is beyond our understanding. Hence, the Word revealed, "…without faith, it is impossible to please God because anyone who comes to Him must believe that He exists and that He rewards those who earnestly seek him" (Hebrews 11:6).

Countless people question the Word of God and rely on different styles or forms of rituals that make sense to them. We want to understand life and live in ways that please us. Most of us are led by our emotions and feelings and tend to forget that we have a creator. "So, God created man in His own image, in the…male and female created He them…And God saw everything that he had made, and, behold, it was very good" (Genesis 1:27–31). There are many debates about life and many different theories and kinds of research on how to make our existence better. However, we forget who the foundation of all things is.

In the late 1960s and 1970s, the notion of "pronoia" was introduced by a singer, and according to American poet, essayist, and political activist John Perry Barlow, the universe is working on your behalf. In the 1990s the term pronoia resurfaced, and in 2005 the author Brezsny put an emphasis on the Word pronoia when he wrote his book *Pronoia Is the Antidote for Paranoia: How the Whole World Is Conspiring to Shower You with Blessings.*

Pronoia is the new slogan for many who refuse to acknowledge God's purpose for our lives and His existence. Countless people accept the idea of pronoia because it helps them to stay optimistic about life and because it boosts their self-confidence and hope. However, to believers in Christ, the book is dark, filled with astrology and many images that can either frighten or play games with the mind.

Because we tend to believe in what our senses can perceive, some people would rather hold on to that perception and negate what is real and forever lasting, which is the Word of God. According to Saillens (2006) "Faith is illumination, conviction, acceptance, and transformation, in addition, faith is a natural fact that is presented through our heart, our reason and conscience" (p. 51). Additionally, for that faith to be active, it does require some work: "Faith without works is dead" (James 2:20). In their inspiring journey of challenges, fear, and faith, Pastors Jim and Dawn Raley (2013) reported that "Faith is a substance." For example, when we hold on to a receipt, when we are waiting for an item to arrive, we have an assurance that the product is on the way. It is also true in prayer; God promises to answer our prayers. By believing Him, your faith becomes substance. Moreover, they say faith is also "evidence" (p. 15).

"For the Word of God is living and powerful, and sharper than any two-edged sword, piercing even to the division of the soul and spirit, and of joints and marrow, and is a discerner of the thoughts and intents of the heart" (Hebrews 4:12). Believers are aware of the power there is when they start talking, praising and praying to God. Nevertheless, the enemy chooses fear and guilt to disarm us from what should be a natural response to any circumstances in our lives. When Jesus was entering Jerusalem as a king, the crowd started to sing, and the Pharisees asked Jesus to rebuke them. Jesus' response was, "If they keep quiet, the stones will cry out" (Luke 19:39-40). We need to start speaking to whatever situation in our daily lives to get the result and the victory that is already ours. As we start to understand whose we are and God's promises for every one of us, we will be walking towards the light with hope, determination, power, authority and most of all, conviction. Faith is a daily challenge that believers need to rely on when they have nowhere to go or when they have little control of a situation, "Fear not, for I am with you, be not dismayed, for I am your God. I will strengthen you, Yes, I will help you, I will uphold you with My righteous right hand" (Isaiah 41: 10). The Word of God brings comfort and hope; a stable force and refuge that surpasses all intelligence. How can one live without?

1. Root and Definition of the Word "Faith"

The Word "faith" comes from the Greek Word "pistis," which means "belief". Additionally, *The Merriam-Webster Dictionary* defines "faith" as a strong belief or trust in someone or something. Faith is that special core value and unshaken hope that beats all the odds. Faith can also be defined as a powerful force that gives one the ability to imagine the impossible that transform lives and gives wings to fly over all circumstances. Faith is the eye of a blind, the words of the mute, the ears of the death. Faith is the foundation for every action and an irrevocable transition to a higher dimension. When it comes to proof, believers know for sure that if they are still standing and living, it is only by the grace of God. Their lives alone are a testimony that their faith is real and proven true by the Word of God. Moreover, the Word of God reveals, "Now faith is confidence in what we hope for and assurance about what we do not see. This is what the ancients were commended for. By faith, we understand that the universe was formed at God's command, so that what is seen was not made out of what was visible (Hebrews11: 1-3).

In addition, when Jesus visited the disciples after His resurrection, Thomas was not among them. When Thomas returned, and they were reporting that they saw the Lord, he refused to believe unless he could put his hands and finger where the nails were. Jesus told Thomas, "Because you have

37

seen me, you have believed; blessed are those who have not seen and yet have believed" (John 20:29). We, believers, can still experience the presence of the Lord through the Holy Spirit because He lives in us. "And I will ask the Father, and he will give you another advocate to help you and be with you forever, the Spirit of truth. The world cannot accept him because it neither sees him nor knows him. But you know him, for he lives with you and will be in you. I will not leave you as orphans; I will come to you. Before long, the world will not see me anymore, but you will see me. Because I live, you also will live" (John 14: 16 -19). Those Words are not empty promises.

2. The Challenges of Faith

Being faithful is much easier to do when things fall into place when all is well, the children listen and are in good health, both parents are working, and we are not lacking anything. When friends and extended family are moving forward and enjoying life, it is easy to believe. However, when we feel the sun doesn't shine on our territory and we are facing problems and trials daily, faith seems to be a hard notion to comprehend. More than ever we need to stand in faith when life is still a hard pill to swallow, when we experience our dreams only in our sleep, and when as much as we pray and stay confident in the Word things don't go our way. Dr. Youssef reported, "The Christian faith is much deeper than faith in a theology or belief system, it is trust in God the Father, who through Christ gives us the courage to trust in Him even when we cannot see" (p. 20). Faith is a day-by-day renewal of the mind and a quotidian reminder that "I can do all things through Christ who strengthens me" (Philippians 4:13).

When we allow ourselves to believe and to experiment with God's eternal love and mercy where there seems to be no hope, we gather a better notion of what it takes to fully commit to Him. The challenges of faith are to let go and to stay still. One of the prayer warriors in the group sentinels mentioned One of the challenges for many is that *"faith has no plan B"*. A plan that is built on the rock that is the Word of God is secured, confirmed, given, and received. "For whatever is born of God overcomes the world. And this is the victory that has overcome the world our faith" (1 John 5:4).

3. Galileo Galilei

Sometimes we do believe that all things are possible. However, when we decide to share our ideas and spend time with those who lack faith, instead of enlightening them, unfortunately, many times we join them in their disbelief. As believers, we need to know that Jesus Christ died on the cross, and because of this sacrifice, we have eternal life. Hence, nothing in this world can hinder us from believing that if we are still alive, it is because of this selfless act. Believers need to have absolute confidence in our knowledge! Jesus died to give us eternal life. Hence, we can be ready and willing to die for what we believe because what we believe is the eternal truth. "Through God, we will do valiantly, for it is He who shall tread down our enemies" (Psalm 60:12). By faith, we have the abundant life and the victory that He provides. The victory is already ours, but the enemy is using his tricks of doubt to hinder you from getting to your destiny. Don't let him. The judgment for Satan is hell. He lost the war, and he is miserable and lonely. As they say, "Misery loves company." Hence, listen to the Word of God, "Blessed is the one who does not walk in step with the wicked or stand in the way that sinners take or sit in the company of mockers, but whose delight is in the law of the Lord, and who meditates on his Law Day and night" (Psalm 1:1–2).

There was a man in the sixteenth century who had a belief that was contrary to what the world believed. Yet, he was willing to die for that belief. The father of modern Science, Galileo Galilei, was in the medical field when he deviated from medicine to mathematics. That diversion allowed him to discover that the earth is not stationary, and it turns around the sun. One of the staff of the History Channel wrote, "After being forced during his trial to admit that the Earth was the stationary center of the universe, Galileo allegedly muttered, '*Eppur si muove!*' ('Yet it moves!')" (History, June 2016). As true or unbelievable the story of Galileo is. We, believers should not fear what is to come, because we know who is the first and who is the last. How many of us are ready and willing to die for what we believe, for the cause of the gospel? To know where we stand, it is crucial to balance our faith.

Galileo displayed a level of belief that we should experience and live by, which is unconditional faith based on knowing the Word of God and believing that we are not alone. Most of us are ready to follow what the majority has to say even though they may be wrong; we struggle with the truth. Remember, the word of the Apostle Paul to the Romans "And do not be conformed to this world, but be transformed by the renewing of your mind, that you may prove what is that good and acceptable and perfect will of God". (Romans 12:2).

Yet, the One who is the truth, the light, and the way is up for grab, but we refuse to open our eyes to see, reach our hand to touch and open our faith to believe that all shall pass but the Word of God! There is nothing that we need we cannot access through faith.

CHAPTER VII
G. TYPES AND LEVELS OF FAITH

1. Total Surrender

Being able to surrender all and not live by sight is one of the first signs of faith. When we spend time with the Lord, we can create an atmosphere of intimacy, and He can reveal Himself to us. Faith can only be experienced when we keep our eyes on the Lord. Peter saw Jesus walking on water, and he wanted to walk toward Him. "Come," he said. Then Peter got down out of the boat, walked on the water and came toward Jesus. But when he saw the wind, he was afraid and, beginning to sink, cried out, "Lord, save me!" Immediately Jesus reached out his hand and caught him. "You of little faith," he said, why did you doubt?" (Matthew 14:29–31).

There are a variety of prayer lines where some men and women set time aside to pray together for the country, children in the community, and one another. Those prayer warriors start as early as 4:00 am in the morning which is a special and powerful time to search and encounter God's presence and to contemplate His face. One of the women was inspired by the Holy Ghost and while thanking God for His gratefulness, the highs and the lows, she stated, "La fwa mwen nan Bondye bay lapé, la fwa mwen nan Bondye bay lavi'm yon lot koulé," which means, "My Faith in the Lord gives peace, my Faith in the Lord brings joy in my life" (Sentinels, 2016). You can also say those Words over your life or your family; if you dare to believe, in His name, it will be done.

The story of Jabez in the Bible reminds us that when we ask with hope and belief, we are more likely to receive God's blessings even though our life seems without a bright future. The name of Jabez means suffering when his mom gave birth to him, she suffered so much that she called him Jabez. Our names always have some story or a meaning behind them.

Even when our names suggest a certain destiny that might be negative, we can still claim and proclaim God's mercy in our lives. "And his mother called his name Jabez, saying, 'Because I bore him in pain.' And Jabez called on the God of Israel saying, 'Oh that you would bless me indeed, and enlarge my territory, that your hand would be with me, and that you would keep me from evil, that I may not cause pain!' So, God granted him what he requested" (1 Chronicles 4:9–10). Yes, through Him, all things are possible. "Therefore, I say to you, whatever things you ask when you pray, believe that you receive them, and you will have them" (Mark 11:24).

While the Word of God is real, direct and is the truth, the enemy tends to use doubt to manipulate our thoughts and emotions. Jeffrey Delva (2018), one of my youth members at NJBChurch was preaching and stated, "*one of the devil's strongest and most powerful tactics is to get us to doubt God's existence and God's promise*". We can clearly see this message been played out during human fall in the Garden of Eden. Now the serpent was craftier than any of the wild animals the Lord God had made. He said to the woman, "Did God really say, 'You must not eat from any tree in the garden'?" The woman said to the serpent, "We may eat fruit from the trees in the garden, but God did say, 'You must not eat fruit from the tree that is in the middle of the garden, and you must not touch it, or you will die." "You will not certainly die," the serpent said to the woman, "For God knows that when you eat from it your eyes will be opened, and you will be like God, knowing good and evil." When the woman saw that the fruit of the tree was good for food and pleasing to the eye, and desirable for gaining wisdom, she took some and ate it. She also gave some to her husband, who was with her, and he ate it. (Genesis 3:1-6).

Delva (2018) continued to say "to doubt is to feel uncertain about something, hesitant and questioning it. The process of doubting can be positive if you come out of it with a stronger faith than ever". Unfortunately, it was not the case for our first parents. They let their doubt question the truth and later realized that *"The truth never changes but lies do"* (Présumé Calixte, 2018). Science is always changing but God is consistent and reliable. Hence, when we have doubts, seek God.

2. Level of Faith Identified by Many.

Blind Faith is faith that has no evidence, no real logic, or detailed foundation. That is not the faith that most believers witness or depend on. We know for sure through God's promises and Word, "I am the way, the truth, and the life. No one comes to the Father except through me" (John 14:6). We learn to move from darkness to light and to grow and to mature in Jesus's name, "For we know in part and we prophesy in part, but when completeness comes, what is in part disappears. When I was a child, I talked like a child, I thought like a child, I reasoned like a child. When I became a man, I put the ways of childhood behind me. For now, we see only a reflection as in a mirror; then we shall see face to face. Now I know in part; then I shall know fully, even as I am fully known. And now these three remain: faith, hope and love. But the greatest of these is love" (1 Corinthians 13: 9 -13).

Weak faith teaches us that faith is a process, a journey that requires daily practice. Hence, we have a responsibility toward those who need support and spiritual growth, and they will need to be strong in the Lord. "He gives strength to the weary and to him who lacks might He increases power" (Isaiah 40:29). "Accept the one whose faith is weak, without quarreling over disputable matters. One person's faith allows them to eat anything, but another, whose faith is weak, eats only vegetables. The one who eats everything must not treat with contempt the one who does not, and the one who does not eat everything must not judge the one who does, for God has accepted them." (Romans 14:1-3).

Christian faith rests on knowledge of God, his character and attributes. There are so many of those traits that are beyond our own understanding and ability to perceive. Most of those qualities belong to Him alone and do not share those traits with anyone. He is Eternal, meaning there is nothing before or after Him. He is I AM. (Exodus 3:14) And God said to Moses, "I AM WHO I AM." Christians rely on the unconditional love and transcendence of Jesus Christ. He is not like anyone that we ever met and will never be able to understand the things that He does and how or why He chooses to act the way He chooses to. He is Mercy, Righteousness in all that He does. Psalm 19:7-9 stated "The law of the Lord is perfect, converting the soul; the testimony of the Lord is sure, making wise the simple; the statutes of the Lord are right, rejoicing the heart; the commandment of the Lord is pure, enlightening the eyes; the fear of the Lord is clean, enduring forever; the judgments of the Lord are true and righteous altogether".

Jeremiah 23:24 "Can a man hide himself in hiding places, So I do not see him?" declares the LORD "Do I not fill the heavens and the earth?" declares the LORD. The Immutability and Self-Existence of God is worth mentioning because as much as we seek to understand and make sense of His existence we lost track of who we are. James 1:17 "Every good thing given, and every perfect gift is from above, coming down from the Father of lights, with whom there is no variation or shifting shadow". Through a lifespan of grace, many have spoken and shared the powerful testimony of knowing Him at different levels and stages by discovering the layers and depths of who God is. "Praise be to the LORD, the God of Israel, who with his own hand has fulfilled what he promised with his own mouth to my father David" (1 Kings 8:15). Understanding God's plan for our lives is essential to trusting him and putting our faith in him without being fickle, because we know he is not a liar.

This type of faith is not based on emotions or temporary events. It is anchored, and it does not vacillate. Abraham was considered a great man of faith for "Abraham in hope believed and so became the father of many nations...Without weakening in his faith, he faced the fact that his body was as good as dead since he was about a hundred years old and that Sarah's womb was also dead. Yet he did not waver through unbelief regarding the promise of God but was strengthened in his faith and gave glory to God...it was credited to him as righteousness" (Romans 4:18-22). Having been exposed to such genuine trustworthiness, one feels compelled to trust and obey.

When speaking of faith, the Bible compares the level of faith with meat and vegetable consumption. This is to discourage unproductive arguments or quarrels among believers. "One person's faith allows them to eat anything, but another, whose faith is weak, eats only vegetables. The one who eats everything must not treat with contempt the one who does not, and the one who does not eat everything must not judge the one who does, for God has accepted them" (Romans 14:2-3). Paul teaches believers to be mindful of quarrels among us. He understands just as we should understand that some of us are baby Christians and need our patience and support, not judgment. It is so easy for those of us who are mature Christians to expect too much from the ones who are new in the faith. The time will come when new Christians will grow strong and mature enough to deal with more complex teaching and sins, but until then we must agree to say, "I gave you milk, not solid food, for you were not yet ready for it. Indeed, you are still not ready" (1 Corinthians 3:2).

Once the new Christian is ready to tackle stronger issues, then with the steady increase in faith and spiritual maturity, he or she too will go from liquid to solid food. We are not our own masters. Therefore, "We who are strong ought to bear with the failings of the weak and not to please ourselves" (Romans 15:1).

Great faith is the level of maturity that not many of us are able to reach but that is needed through Christian lives. "Then Jesus answered and said to her, 'O woman, great is your faith! Let it be to you as you desire.' And her daughter was healed from that very hour" (Matthew 15:28).

Dead faith is when we want things to happen for us like magic and with this, we fail to sacrifice the time in prayer and we avoid doing God's work, "For as the body without the spirit is dead, so faith without works is dead also" (James 2:26). Some of us lost faith because some of our prayers were not answered during our expected time. We forgot that God is never late. "The Lord is not slack concerning His promise, as some men count slackness, but is longsuffering toward us, not willing that any should perish, but that all should come to repentance" (2 Peter 3:9).

Genuine faith is when we wake up and continue our day-to-day life and unconsciously believe that we will see tomorrow. Through our praise and prayers, we can show God how much we believe in His name and compassion. "That the genuineness of your faith, being much more precious than gold that perishes, though it is tested by fire, may be found to praise, honor, and glory at the revelation of Jesus Christ" (1 Peter 1:7).

Salvation faith refers to the fact that we know for sure that if we are saved, it is not by our own doing but by God's grace. "Nor is there salvation in any other, for there is no other name under heaven given among men by which we must be saved" (Acts 4:12).

Faith in action indicates that faith is an action Word; we need to prove our faith because it is being tested daily. When you have received a Word from God, keep prophesizing those Words over your life, your family, your circumstances until you see it comes to past. The enemy's plan is to rob your joy, hence continue to praise when sorrow may come your way. If the saying is true, "that action speaks louder than Word"? We need to start holding on to the promise, regardless of the trials and start to praise again, rejoice in the Lord because God will do whatever he said he would do. Shout victory in His name, dance before the Lord for the battle is won. Sing a new song because you have overcome, Halleluiah! Then he said to me, "This is what the Lord says to Zerubbabel: It is neither by force nor by strength, but by my Spirit, says the Lord of Heaven's Armies". (Zechariah 4:6).

All Christians share a common faith, shared by all who believe that mankind can only find salvation through Jesus Christ, the Messiah. Paul refers to that faith as "mutual faith." "That is, that I may be encouraged together with you by the mutual faith both of you and me" (Romans 1:12).

3.   The Test of Faith

Our faith is tested daily. For many of us, our faith is tested through unemployment or at the hospital with a sick child, through difficulties with a friend, trials in marital relationships. When all is well, suddenly the rain of sorrows and calamities start pouring and refuse to stop. Our faith will be tested, as any student ought to pass an exam to test their understanding of any subject a child under the debris of a house, a disease that has no treatment, or a business that is failing regardless of our hard work. What we do and stand for in times of challenge can build and strengthen our faith. The real problem comes when we begin to doubt ourselves and our abilities to succeed. Worst yet, we begin to doubt God and his power and promises. We tend to forget that our lives and where we are going are in His hands. He told us, "Come to Me, all you who labor and are heavy laden, and I will give you rest. Take My yoke upon you and learn from Me, for I am gentle and lowly in heart, and you will find rest for your souls. For My yoke is easy and My burden is light" (Matthew 11:28-29). Division comes over simple and silly things; the type of food to eat or the type of music we listen to. Sometimes, when faith is most needed we fail to exhibit our true conviction in the Word and our will to let go and to let God lead. "When God leads you to the edge of the cliff, trust Him fully and let go. Only one of two things will happen: either He'll catch you when you fall, or He'll teach you how to fly (Unknown, 2014).

Many before us have been tested, and the only difference between us and them is their total faith and humility to the idea that when they can't, God can. When it is too much, too hard to swallow, or too difficult to make sense of, there is always someone who can handle it all. To pass the test of faith, it requires total reliance on the only God and to remind ourselves as the singer Bob Marley and the Wailers sang it so well "Everything is going to be alright." Furthermore, "But he who doubts is condemned if he eats, because he does not eat from faith; for whatever is not from faith is sin" (Romans 14:29). Let us build on the faith that sees beyond the mountains and the valleys. Faith that is deep-rooted in hope, belief, higher standard and expectations from the One who has made us will never forsake us; especially when things are too harsh to swallow.

CHAPTER VIII
H. MEN AND WOMEN OF FAITH IN THE BIBLE

Through prayers, we can meet with God and access the realm of blessings. Hence, it will be misleading to not mention how some influential men and women in the Bible have decided to be in a constant communication and in an intimate relationship with God while living a faithful life. Being faithful is no easy task, but through God's grace and mercy, when we learn to surrender all to Him and have a strong conviction that God can only give us wings to fly or reveal Himself to us and make things that seems impossible turns into possible.

We will look at a few of those men and women in the Bible whose stories can bring better understanding and a great influence in our daily lives. Our stories are so similar to what some of those people dealt with, and maybe there are lessons for us to learn. Those men and women are a reminder that life will have many challenges, but with unconditional love and belief in the Word of God, we in return can have victory over all things. Those people were influential and victorious not because of what they did but because of their faith.

1. Abraham

It would be bewildering not to mention the first man of faith, the father of all generations. Abraham and his walk with God was a true manifestation of commitment, hope, and incredible faith that can only be experienced by those who truly believe. How would you react after going through so much in your life and leaving your home, holding on to just a promise? A promise from God is a blessing, a gift that one can touch and taste without seeing. Abraham had a clear vision and knowledge about a God who told him to leave his home. He also had great faith that allowed him to believe that he would be the father of all nations even though he did not have a child at the time. Abraham's faith was beyond understanding, so much so that it touched the life of Sara, his wife, in ways that only total blind faith could offer. Sara was unable to understand what was going on in her life; she thought people would be laughing at her story, but when she was old, sterile, and a stranger, the promise of God for Abraham remained true in her life. Their journey reminds us that the promise of God is to wait in patience because no one can stop or block God, the Almighty. God can make things possible when things seem scientifically, humanely and socially impossible.

Sara was ninety years old when she gave a son to Abraham. The story and the faith of Abraham went even further. After God finally blessed him and his wife with a son called Isaac. Later, he was asked by God to give that promised child as a sacrifice. How many of us would consult God over and over in such circumstances? How many of us would question: Are you sure, God?! Many would stop listening to God. Abraham did something that most of us refuse to do, which is to obey. Furthermore, he did not only obey, but it was an obedience without understanding and he followed through. "By faith Abraham, when God tested him, offered Isaac as a sacrifice. He who had embraced the promises was about to sacrifice his one and only son, even though God had said to him, 'It is through Isaac that your offspring will be reckoned'" (Hebrews 11:17-18).

By believing without seeing or understanding God's way, Abraham chose to put his trust in the Lord. "By faith Abraham, when called to go to a place he would later receive as his inheritance, obeyed and went, even though he did not know where he was going. By faith he made his home in the promised land like a stranger in a foreign country; he lived in tents, as did Isaac and Jacob, who were heirs with him of the same promise. For he was looking forward to the city with foundations, whose architect and builder is God." (Hebrews 11:8 -10). Although it is fair to ask questions, the believer needs to reach that point of understanding that God has control over our lives. If we truly believe, when challenges come our way we need to surrender all to Him.

In our minuscule minds, we are unable to understand God's plan for our lives. "For my thoughts are not your thoughts, neither are your ways my ways, declares the LORD. As the heavens are higher than the earth, so are my ways higher than your ways and my thoughts than your thoughts" (Isaiah 55:8-9). We need to be in a place of total surrender to God's will to be done in our lives. God has proven His unconditional love for us on the cross, so we can have life and walk by faith and not by sight.

2. Noah and the Ark

The story of Noah testifies not only to the glory and the compassion of the Lord but also to the idea that we should not live by sight but by faith. Whenever we are in a unique position to hear a Word from the Lord, we need to receive it and build on those Words because it is against God's nature to lie. When we hear his voice, we have a responsibility to respond and to act on His Word, "For many are called, but few are chosen" (Matthew 22:14). When we start living a life built on the Word of God, people can ridicule us, and they may think that we are out of our minds. "By faith Noah, when warned about things not yet seen, in holy fear built an ark to save his family. By his faith he condemned the world and became heir of the righteousness that is in keeping with faith." (Hebrews11:7). We are fortunate when we believe to the fullest and know that God is in control of our lives, this we can listen and follow his command. Therefore, we should not be concerned about what people may think or even say to or about us. "The message of the cross is foolish to those who are headed for destruction, but we who are being saved know it is the very power of God" (1 Corinthians 1:18).

The lesson that is to be learned from the story of Noah is the same in this new era or new generation. Whenever God speaks, we must listen even nature obeys to His Word because He is our creator. "The disciples went and woke him, saying, 'Master, Master, we're going to drown!' He got up and rebuked the wind and the raging waters; the storm subsided, and all was calm. 'Where is your faith?' he asked his disciples. In fear and amazement, they asked one another, 'Who is this? He commands even the winds and the water, and they obey him' (Luke 8:24-25). Noah's conviction is a testament of his faith. Noah's belief is an element of surprise for the nonbelievers. At times people may ridicule our dreams or think little of where we are heading. Since God's Word cannot come back void, we should walk with confidence, irrevocable hope and faith that His Word will come to past. Noah revealed to us God's compassion, authenticity and His amazing nature through unchangeable faith! "But you remain the same, and your years will never end." (Psalms 102: 27).

3. Joseph

The story of Joseph is a story of despair, but one full of hope and commitment to the Word and promise of the Lord. We need to live a life of conviction, and we need to have an assurance that God has full control and authority over our lives, regardless of what comes against us. At a young age, Joseph knew in his heart he was different from his brothers. Even though he was the youngest of all his siblings, he had a natural gift, the gift of dream, of prophecy; God revealed mysteries to him in his dreams because he was the chosen one.

He was not only someone who could dream but someone who had the ability to understand the meaning of anyone's dream. Joseph shared one of his dreams with his brothers. "He said to them, "Listen to this dream I had: We were binding sheaves of grain out in the field when suddenly my sheaf rose and stood upright, while your sheaves gathered around mine and bowed down to it"" (Genesis 37:6-7). Once Joseph shared his story with his siblings, jealousy, hatred, and even the desire to kill him possessed their minds. Joseph was so in tune with his dreams that he kept on sharing those dreams as a testimony of who he was. "'Listen,' he said, 'I had another dream, and this time the sun and moon and eleven stars were bowing down to me." When he told his father as well as his brothers, his father rebuked him and said: "What is this dream you had? Will your mother and I and your brothers come and bow down to the ground before you? His brothers were jealous of him, but his father kept the matter in mind" (Gen 37:9-11).

Believers ought to keep dreaming and take time to write about some of the visions God reveals to us. Additionally, to keep on believing that dreams can become reality. For example, Joseph's brothers sold him because they were unable to kill him. At times, we complain when we fail to get the result expected or having or our wish granted in our scheduled time. We forget that our Savior is never late, and His timing is always perfect. Therefore, more than ever, we should remember "All things work together for good to them that love God, to them who are the called according to his purpose" (Romans 8:28). Joseph was ridiculed as a dreamer, but there is nothing wrong with dreams and aspirations. As opposed to worrying about those around us, it is crucial that we remember to always keep our eyes on Jesus because He said, "I will lead the blind by ways they have not known, along unfamiliar paths I will guide them; I will turn the darkness into light before them and make the rough places smooth. These are the things I will do; I will not forsake them" (Isaiah 42:16).

Even though Joseph was sold by his brothers because of their insecurities and thrown away into jail for things that he had not committed, "The LORD was with him, he showed him kindness and granted him favor in the eyes of the prison warden" (Genesis 39:21). Joseph stayed true to his God and judgment and never once stopped having faith in God. Pharaoh had a dream, and the only one who could interpret that dream was Joseph. This portion of the story should be a reminder to us all; God has given us power, authority, and other skills that are ingrained inside of us. God is waiting for the right time for His name to be glorified and for the world to know that He is God, and His plan cannot be differed due to the circumstances in our lives.

Pharaoh said to Joseph, "I had a dream, and no one can interpret it. But I have heard it said of you that when you hear a dream you can interpret it." Sometimes, a stranger can recognize and perceive that we have been granted something that is beyond the usual. Because Pharaoh heard, he instantly believes. He believes that Joseph has been given a special talent, an amazing gift that is beyond anything that he ever witnessed, and it can only be from God. Joseph who knew his ability is rooted in God replied to Pharaoh, "I cannot do it," … "but God will give Pharaoh the answer he desires" (Genesis 41:15-16).

We need to mirror Joseph's faith in God and surrender totally to His power. Joseph knew that he could not do anything on his own, but that through God, all things are possible. Grace and favor have been given to us for free, not that we are deserving of them but because God is love, compassion, mercy, and an amazing provider. When we are in a place of despair and feeling lost and discouraged, when no one else can come to our rescue, our God can, and He will. By activating our confidence and faith in the Lord, we can see and experience the wonders of His mighty name. Joseph's journey taught us that God can make a way when everything seems final or impossible. Joseph's story is a reminder that God never forsake his children and His Word never comes back to Him void. The story of Joseph may look like yours let us rely on His plan and holding on to our dream. Joseph did not compromise his faith when tempted either, he would rather go to jail and believe that sooner or later that God will make a way. Do you believe that God can make a way in your incomprehensible situation?

4. Job

During the financial crisis, many identified with the story of Job. How many of us had the courage to blame God when we had done all we should have done, and yet we lost everything? Job was a rich man. He had all he wanted or all he could wish for. "Also, his possessions were seven thousand sheep, three thousand camels, five hundred yokes of oxen, five hundred female donkeys, and a very large household, so that this man was the greatest of all the people of the East" (Job 1:3). Regardless of his wealth, friends, family, and health, there was something greater than anything else that he had, which was a relationship with the Lord. Job trusted God, and he trusted Him to the fullest. Hence, when Satan dared to ask God about Job, God granted his wish. "Does Job fear God for nothing? Have you not made a hedge around him, around his household, and around all that he has on every side? You have blessed the work of his hands, and his possessions have increased in the land. But now, stretch out Your hand and touch all that he has, and he will surely curse You to Your face!" And the Lord said to Satan, "Behold, all that he has is in your power; only do not lay a hand on his person" (Job 1:9-12).

In the current situation that we are facing, we ought to believe that the Lord believes in us; hence, we must share the same faith. Those challenges must force us to think that "Why me?" but it should be "Why not me?" God believes in us, and we need to be in a place to comprehend that money, spouses, children, and all the world has to offer will pass, but His grace and mercy is everlasting. Accordingly, our relationship with the Lord should stand in great foundation, so when trials come our way, we know that our faith will see us through. When friends, family, wealth, and Job had were gone, he remained faithful even though what was happening in his life did not make any sense. He kept the faith as opposed to feeling sorry for himself. He stated: "Naked I came from my mother's womb, and naked shall I return there. The Lord gave, and the Lord has taken away; blessed be the name of the Lord" (Job 1:21). How many of us can hold on to faith and not waver when we do not understand and endure in faith? Can God bet on you?

We need to fight a good fight and remain in an attitude of recognition, having conviction, and gratefulness to find a way to worship when the enemy is trying to hurt us. Among all, God is still present. We may not understand, but God is still alive and is still looking forward to bless us with spiritual gifts and amazing grace because "This I recall to my mind, therefore have I hope. It is of the Lord's mercies that we are not consumed, because his compassions fail not. They are new every morning: great is thy faithfulness" (Lamentations 3:21-23). As we recall in praise and prayer we can see Him move mountains. "I've seen you move, you move the mountains, and I believe you'll do it over again" (Elevation Worship, 2017).

5. Joshua and the Wall of Jericho

There are some battles in our lives that we will win through silence, and when it is our due time, we will make a noise of Halleluiah and shout, "Only you, God, Only you!" Claiming victory and freedom even though it is out of our reach should be the life of a believer. When God spoke to Joshua, He said, "See, I have delivered Jericho into your hands, along with its king and fighting men. March around the city once with all the armed men…On the seventh day, march around the city seven times, with the priests blowing the trumpets. When you hear them sound a long blast on the trumpets, have the whole army give a loud shout; then the wall of the city will collapse, and the army will go up, everyone straight in" (Joshua 6:2-5). In silence, keeping our eyes on the Lord, sometimes that is how we can win some of our battles. As Moses told the people, "The LORD will fight for you; you need only to be still" (Exodus 14:14).

Sometimes we are unable to win some of the battles of our lives because we think we should talk, or we must share what is in our mind. Sometimes, most of the challenges can be won by a simple silence. As the saying goes, "*Silence is golden.*" "Even fools are thought wise if they keep silent, and discerning if they hold their tongues" (Proverbs17: 28).

6. David

Many of us can relate to David due to the many challenges he faced as a man and the decisions he made carelessly or by pure emotions or feelings. One great advantage David had was a sincere heart and the acknowledgement of his wrongdoing. David also had a thankful heart, he could recall who God is, and remembered how He had been with him while taking care of his father's sheep. Therefore, it is by faith that David responded to Goliath and believed in God's favor for victory. … "You come against me with sword and spear and javelin, but I come against you in the name of the Lord Almighty, the God of the armies of Israel, whom you have defied. This day the Lord will deliver you into my hands, and I'll strike you down and cut off your head. This very day I will give the carcasses of the Philistine army to the birds and the wild animals, and the whole world will know that there is a God in Israel. All those gathered here will know that it is not by sword or spear that the Lord saves; for the battle is the Lord's, and he will give all of you into our hands" (1 Samuel 17:45-47). What a name!

How many of us have the courage and the faith needed to talk to their situation and rely on the mercy and faithfulness of the Lord? David knew and believed that there is power in the name of Jesus. He also knew, "You shall not misuse the name of the LORD your God, for the LORD will not hold anyone guiltless who misuses his name" (Exodus 20:7). Most of all, David did not take any credit for himself but gave glory to the Highest. Many times, in our daily lives there are some situations that may seem impossible and difficult to overcome. This story of David is a reminder that the Word "impossible" does not belong in God's Kingdom. "The voice of the LORD twists the oaks and strips the forests bare. And in his temple, all cry, "Glory!" (Psalm 29:9). Today God is still seeking for some "David's" who are willing to praise Him when all seems lost and despair comes their way.

David had the courage to count God's blessings in his life, as he was calculating each step. He also knew that he needed to praise God during his adversity for he understood that His God was (and is) greater than the challenges he faced. Therefore, we can establish that there is no one else like God. Hence, he commanded his soul, all that he had, and all that he possessed to praise God. "Bless the Lord, O my soul; And all that is within me, bless His holy name! Bless the Lord, O my soul" (Psalm103:1-2). David's call to his soul was a form of gratitude towards God. He let go of all his emotions, his spirit, and his body to sing and dance before the Lord. We need to have that same gratitude and faith to say, "I will lift up my eyes to the hills from whence comes my help? My help comes from the Lord, Who made heaven and earth" (Psalm 21:1-2).

Where does your strength and courage come from when all seems lost? If we apply our faith when we are weak, He can carry us through the dark times. If we rely on His power, we can be strong and sing in the eye of adversities. If we decide to follow Him and to live for God while loving, believing in His plan for our lives, a smile should emerge on our faces when the enemy tries to destroy the plan that the Lord has for us. David believed, and so can we.

7. Shadrach, Meshach, and Abed-Nego

Those three young Hebrews, Shadrach, Meshach, and Abed-Nego, occupied a great place in the kingdom of Nebuchadnezzar. As Daniel, they were also deportees. They were ready to die for the Lord when they told the King Nebuchadnezzar that they cannot serve its gods, nor would they worship the gold image that the king sets up. When someone dared to defy the king, there was a huge consequence. "And he commanded certain mighty men of valor who were in his army to bind Shadrach, Meshach, and Abed-Nego, and cast them into the burning fiery furnace" (Daniel 3:20). Their faith in the Lord delivered them from the burning fiery furnace. Moreover, there are some situations that we face sometimes when God Himself comes to restore our hope and belief by reminding us that we are not alone. God is waiting for us to make a stand. God is waiting for us to represent Him as the salt and the light in this world of craziness. If we do not stand for Him, how can we experience who He is? "Whosoever therefore shall confess me before men, him will I confess also before my Father which is in heaven. But whosoever shall deny me before men, him will I also deny before my Father which is in heaven" (Matthew 10:32-33).

The story of Shadrach, Meshach and Abed-Nego is still significant today for all of us. We must surround ourselves with

Christians so that we can stay grounded in the Word. "Blessed is the one who does not walk in step with the wicked or stand in the way that sinners take or sit in the company of mockers, but whose delight is in the law of the Lord, and who meditates on his Law Day and night. That person is like a tree planted by streams of water, which yields its fruit in season and whose leaf does not wither- whatever they do prospers" (Psalm 1:1-3).

The bond that connected those friends was their faith that they had in the Lord. Even though they had changed their names and they had learned different languages and a new culture, they stayed true to whom they were. They had given everything they had, and the only thing they were unable to let go of was their faith in the Lord. They recognized that there is one God. Their commitment, conviction, and their conduct are a model for all of us to follow. Additionally, the scripture provides us with comfort. God's Word says: "When you pass through the waters, I will be with you; and through the rivers, they shall not overflow you. When you walk through the fire, you shall not be burned nor shall the flame scorch you" (Isaiah 43:2).

8. Daniel

The Bible teaches us about a man who was faithful to God in all that he undertakes. His name was Daniel. While in exile at a young age, he was one of the three administrators appointed by King Darius, and among those appointed were also 120 satraps. In our journey with the Lord, we will be faced with situations that are beyond our control. Because we are unique and different, people tend to hold grudges against us without our knowledge. It is important to be true to ourselves and to acknowledge that God's plan in our lives will never change regardless of the situations. Many of us are born with the light of God shining inside of us, and therefore no matter

60

what we do or where we go, we will be treated with special favor. "Now Daniel so distinguished himself among the administrators and the satraps by his exceptional qualities that the king planned to set him over the whole kingdom" (Daniel. 6:3). Because Daniel found favor in the eyes of King Darius, it triggered a lot of hate and jealousy among the satraps, and they were trying to eliminate Daniel.

Daniel was trustworthy, and he was not negligent or corrupt. The satraps knew that the only way to have him stripped away from his position was to use the law of his God against him. Hence, "The royal administrators, prefects, satraps, advisers and governors have all agreed that the king should issue an edict and enforce the decree that anyone who prays to any god or human being during the next thirty days, except to you, Your Majesty, shall be thrown into the lions' den" (Daniel 6:7). Daniel knew about the decree and the consequences, yet he continued to pray at least three times a day to the only God that he knew, the God of Israel, who had done marvelous things in his life. Even though it was time to send him in the lion's den, Daniel remained faithful to his God, ready and willing to die for his belief. The scriptures tell us "So the king gave the order and they brought Daniel and threw him into the lions' den. The king said to Daniel "May your God, whom you serve continually, rescue you!" (Daniel 6:16).

Daniel depended on the Lord to be his judge as His name is well defined; even the king was hopeful for him. While in the lions' den, Daniel was safe, and his God prevailed. Sometimes the tools the enemy uses to destroy you can also be the enemy's own sentence. The following day the King visited the den and found out that Daniel was safe. Quickly King Darius understood that Daniel's God is the only God. Because of Daniel's faith, the Word tells us: "Then King Darius wrote to all the nations and peoples of every language in all the earth: "May you prosper greatly! "I issue a decree that in every part of my kingdom people must fear and reverence the God of

Daniel. "For he is the living God and he endures forever; his kingdom will not be destroyed, his dominion will never end. He rescues, and he saves; he performs signs and wonders in the heavens and on the earth. He has rescued Daniel from the power of the lions" (Daniel 6:25-27).

Daniel knew who he was in the Lord, so confident that the Lord called him a man of high esteem. God can still use us today to make a difference in the lives of those who are lost and in despair, those who are enchained in fear and are unable to access faith. Dr. Youssef (2015) stated, "so ghosts of anxiety, unbelief, and doubt, they are not of God. When we experience these emotions, we can know they are distorting our ability to see God, who is there with us in the storm. (p.3). Daniel's story made us realize that when we depend on God truly and faithfully and we are led to the top of the cliff, we must believe one of those two things will happen He will give us wings to fly, or He will catch us when we are falling. When the situation seems desperate, and it is too much to bear, we ought to remember that God is sovereign.

Many immigrants can compare their lives to Daniel's life. Sometimes the enemy knows us and knows our lows and highs, our falls and past sins, but one thing Satan tends to forget is that our God is almighty and powerful, and those who put their faith in Him will never be alone. "For all have sinned and fall short of the glory of God, being justified freely by His grace through the redemption that is in Christ Jesus, whom God set forth as a propitiation by His blood, through faith, to demonstrate His righteousness, because in His forbearance God had passed over the sins that were previously committed" (Romans 3:23-25). When we come to the Lord in prayer and ask for forgiveness, it is done in His name. Hence the enemy cannot use our sins against us anymore. What a consolation!

9. The Faith of the Centurion

Most of us tend to judge people because of the way they look and the things they do. One thing about God is that He does not judge us, He is our advocate, but one day He will be our judge. "My little children, I am writing these things to you so that you may not sin and if anyone sins, we have an Advocate with the Father, Jesus Christ the righteous" (1 John 2:1). Currently, we are under His grace and mercy.

A centurion knew what it meant to be in a position of power. He also knew the meaning and the power that lies in a Word, that came from a powerful person. In a time of distress, he reached out to Jesus. "'Lord,' he said, 'my servant lies at home paralyzed, suffering terribly.' Jesus said to him, 'Shall I come and heal him?' The centurion replied, 'Lord, I do not deserve to have you come under my roof. But just say the Word, and my servant will be healed, for I myself am a man under authority, with soldiers under me. I tell this one, "Go," and he goes, and that one, "Come," and he did come. I say to my servant, "Do this," and he does it.' When Jesus heard this, he was amazed and said to those following him, 'Truly I tell you, I have not found anyone in Israel with such great faith. I say to you that many will come from the east and the west and will take their places at the feast with Abraham, Isaac and Jacob in the kingdom of heaven. But the subjects of the kingdom will be thrown outside, into the darkness, where there will be weeping and gnashing of teeth.' Then Jesus said to the centurion, 'Go! Let it be done just as you believed it would.' And his servant was healed at that moment" (Matthew 8:6-13). We can do all things through Him. How many of us let doubt and uncertainty dominate our lives when the power of faith is right in front of our fingertips? Let us ask, for the Word tells us: "Ask and it will be given to you; seek and you will find; knock and the door will be opened to you. For everyone who asks receives; the one who seeks finds; and to the one who knocks, the door will be opened" (Matthew 7:7-8).

63

10. The Faith of a Canaanite Woman

How many times have we been in situations when even doctors or the savants are unable to give us an answer to our questions or find a solution to our problems? Most of us tend to lose faith because we have no control, or we do not know what to do and where to go. As women, having a child is such a blessing and an honor that we tend to lose our minds when we are unable to help our children in their pains and sufferings. There was a woman who agreed to humiliate herself and agreed to stand in faith to get the needed result for her daughter. "'Lord, Son of David, have mercy on me! My daughter is demon-possessed and suffering terribly.' Jesus did not answer a Word. So, his disciples came to him and urged him, 'Send her away, for she keeps crying out after us.' He answered, 'I was sent only to the lost sheep of Israel.' The woman came and knelt before him. 'Lord, help me!' she said. He replied, 'It is not right to take the children's bread and toss it to the dogs.' 'Yes, it is, Lord,' she said. 'Even the dogs eat the crumbs that fall from their master's table.' Then Jesus said to her, 'Woman, you have great faith! Your request is granted.' And her daughter was healed at that moment" (Matthew 15:22-28).

This dialogue and story should continue to comfort our spirits and help us remember that God has not changed. His love for us has not changed. "The LORD your God in your midst, The Mighty One, will save; He will rejoice over you with gladness, He will quiet you with His love, He will rejoice over you with singing" (Zephaniah 3:17).

11. The Shunammite's Son Restored to Life

As followers of Christ, when tough times come our way, as opposed to sharing our dismay with just anyone or everyone, the best thing is to ask God for discernment. Through God's guidance, we will know where to go and with whom we can share our deepest sorrow with.

The Shunamite woman, while in a time of despair and incomparable pain, believed the same God who agreed to bless her with a child was the one who could restore her son's life. As this woman, we need to be in a position to say, "All is well in God's name"; even though we are on the verge of crying, not everyone needs to know that we are facing distress. "Then she called to her husband and said, 'Send me one of the servants and one of the donkeys that I may quickly go to the man of God and come back again.' And he said, 'Why will you go to him today? It is neither new moon nor Sabbath.' She said, 'All is well'" (2 Kings 4:22-23). This Shunammite's woman did not even say a Word to her husband because she was holding onto hope and faith; knowing that if she can talk to the prophet, all would be just fine. We have learned that when Elisha came, the Shunammite's son life was restored.

God needs a prophet, a servant, and an agent of change. We know that for change to happen, a relationship is necessary, and it must be built on a solid foundation of trust and mutual respect. Our relationship with the Lord is the most powerful weapon that we can use when our challenges seem greater than us. It is only by having an experience and a relationship with God that we can succeed, and we can reach our destiny. However, the enemy tries his best to face us with our fears and our pasts while hindering us from reaching our goals and God's plans in our lives. By strengthening our faith and learning how faith can lead us to our destiny, we will also discover and be reminded of His Word. "And we know that in all things God works for the good of those who love him, who have been called according to his purpose" (Romans 8:28).

12. Ruth

The story of Ruth is beyond understanding. If we were to analyze the logic behind it or try to make sense of the complete trust that she placed in Naomi, it would be difficult to comprehend. After marrying the son of Naomi, Mahlon, misfortune struck Ruth when Mahlon and his brother Chilion who wed Orpah both passed. At that time, Ruth displayed a level of loyalty and devotion to Naomi. More importantly, her faith in God put her in a position to taste the best that life had to offer when hope and the future didn't seem so bright. When Orpah decided to go back to her homeland as Naomi urged her to do so, Ruth refused to leave and said, "Entreat me not to leave you, or to turn back from following you; For wherever you go, I will go; And wherever you lodge, I will lodge; Your people shall be my people, And your God, my God. Where you die, I will die, and there will I be buried. The LORD do so to me, and more also, if anything but death parts you and me" (Ruth 1:16-17).

That is a typical example of faith and total abandonment. This story is embedded with challenges, loyalty, and faith that can be experienced by any of us today when we are led by the Spirit of God.

13. Peter

Peter is one of the most controversial yet, most fascinating disciples of Jesus Christ. Most of us may remember him as the one who denies knowing Jesus Christ and we fail to remember and take notice of the transformation of his mind and heart. Even though he denies Jesus, he shows a level of faith that Thomas and other disciples were unable to display. Peter was a real as you and me, he had weaknesses, a temper and all but God was able to use him for His glory. When Peter realized his mistake he asked for forgiveness, most of us let fear of rejection and guilt hinder us from being in peace with ourselves and to come to the Lord. Peter had many occurrences during his journey on earth that he allowed God to intervene for Him.

Chapter fourteen in the book of Matthew, it explained how Peter's faith allowed him to walk on water but also highlight what doubts and fear can do to us. "... Shortly before dawn Jesus went out to them, walking on the lake. When the disciples saw him walking on the lake, they were terrified. "It's a ghost," they said, and cried out in fear. But Jesus immediately said to them, "Take courage! It is I, don't be afraid." "Lord, if it's you," Peter replied, "tell me to come to you on the water." "Come," he said. Then Peter got down out of the boat, walked on the water and came toward Jesus. But when he saw the wind, he was afraid and, beginning to sink, cried out, "Lord, save me!" Immediately Jesus reached out his hand and caught him. "You of little faith," he said, "why did you doubt?" And when they climbed into the boat, the wind died down. Then those who were in the boat worshiped him, saying, "Truly you are the Son of God." Peter's story did not stop there. Again, after he received the Holy Spirit, he joined John and healed a crippled beggar in the name of Jesus Christ. (Acts 3:19)

More importantly, the faith and the power that Peter exhibited when the Holy Spirit Came at Pentecost is the true definition of authority when we know the power there is in the name of Jesus. Peter stood up with the eleven disciples raised his voice and addressed the crowd; Yes, Peter, the one who denied knowing Jesus, the one who doubted and sank. That day, after talking to the crowd, three thousand accepted Jesus Christ as their personal Savior.

67

What is the difference between our lives and those that are written in and heard from the Bible? Those men and women in the Bible could activate their faith because of their dependence and total surrender to the Lord. I sturdily believe that their connection and involvement were the cornerstones of their relationship with God. The only way to stimulate our faith (as those who were before us) is through the same process of total dependency, of belief without seeing and through holding on to hope that is beyond understanding.

The way we live, the way we talk, and our way of thinking and expressing ourselves should be the legacy for the next generation. That faith needs to be transparent in the way that we handle the journey of our lives as a living testimony of the goodness and God's compassion toward us. That faith should be the legacy for our children and our children's offspring. We are the Daniel's and the Ruth's of this generation. We are here today in this moment to stand up and rise. Rise for the forgotten ones, rise for those who are crippled by fear. Rise, speak, and prophesy that our children will be the head and not the tail, they will prosper, and they will live the abundant life. Moreover, we can stand firm even in the desert because God already made provisions. God can transform the desert in a valley and give His breath. "I will attach tendons to you and make flesh come upon you and cover you with skin; I will put breath in you, and you will come to life. Then you will know that I am the Lord" (Isaiah 37:6). Hence, let us be the ones who are telling others who God is in our daily walk with Him, in the way those we live, and, in the way, we interact with our brothers and sisters.

Through our journey in life with the Lord, how many of us have experienced that same level of faith? If we hold on to Him and His Word truthfully, we can access the keys to not only eternal life, but to the beginning of wisdom and complete surrendering to His will in our lives. We must stay faithful until the end!

Invited to speak at a children's conference at Camp Rumney, in New Hampshire. I was moved by board on a wall; *"Happy moments, praise God. Difficult moments seek God. Quiet moments, worship God. Painful moments, trust God. Every moment, thank God".*

It seems to me, those before us had that saying in their heart and their spirit. There are so many lessons to be learned by the way the saints agreed to serve, obey and trusted God. We understand the nature and level of faith of those servants were based on total reliance and dependency on God. Their faith was rooted in the way they will seek God's in prayer daily as well as having a thankful heart.

CHAPTER IX

I. Faith is

Faith is what we hope for.
Faith is revelation of something no one ever experienced.
Faith is what we have not seen yet believe exists.
Faith is the creative power of God.
Faith is total assurance.
Faith is fundamental armor that is interconnected to hope
Faith is the cancellation of natural laws.
Faith is reliance on the Word of God.
Faith is confidence in the things to come.
Faith is transformed information.
Faith is the lifeblood of Jesus.
Faith is hope in despair.
Faith is the shield of Christians' armor.
Faith is the down payment on God's desire.
Faith is the guarantee of answered prayer.
Faith is God's endless dividend.
Faith is an investment in God that never fails.
Faith is a miracle walk.
Faith is cancellation of the plan of the enemy over your children and the generation to come.
Faith is obedience and boldness.
Faith is doubt free.
Faith is speaking the Word of God.
Faith is an adventure.
Faith is hope and action
Faith is believing without understanding.
Faith is a healthy delusion.
Faith is supernatural truth in God's spoken Word.
Faith is prescription-free medicine for the soul.
Faith is an adventure that promises endurance and maturity.

(Soraya P. Calixte, 2017)

1. Faith Keeps Us Moving Forward

We must agree to fight the good fight and to not just stand because following Him is a sacrifice. Therefore, what is keeping you from moving? People in the business world believe that being persistent, hardworking, consistent, and eager to win are the keys to success. The same rule applies in the realm of faith or in any Christian's life. God didn't say everything will be easy, all that we do requires discipline and commitment. Hence, how do we act or react when we are feeling stuck or put down? We need to hold on to His promise, that he will be with us, always.

When the three young Hebrews agreed to not serve any other gods and were sent in the burning furnace, they were ready to accept it all but also because they believed the God of gods would not forsake them. "God is not a man, one given to lies, and not a son of a man changing his mind" (Numbers 23:19). We, believers, ought to embrace life and what it brings with grace, intelligence and wisdom. The question is, what do we need as opposed to what do we want? Furthermore, life's circumstances reveal to us that what we really need is not necessarily what we thought we wanted. Jacob knew that he needed something greater than what he was used to. While he wrestled with the angel, he was determined to receive a blessing and he would not let the angel leave without blessing him, even though it cost him to limp.

The same is true for all of us who truly believe in the Word of God, "So shall My Word be that goes forth from My mouth; It shall not return to Me void, but it shall accomplish what I please, and it shall prosper in the thing for which I sent it" (Isaiah 51:11). Regardless of what life throws at us, we need to hold on to the Word of God. No matter what challenges we may face, we ought to believe things will get better. As we count our blessings and try our best to reconcile with ourselves and the people around us. It won't be easy; however, we will reach maturity, hope, and the unbreakable will to succeed.

Life will never be just easygoing; there will be wars, tribulations, hatred, heartbreak rainy days, dark moments, dry seasons and turbulences. There will always be a reason to question and experience some types of uncertainties in our lives or those around us. We must hold on to faith because, sooner than later, the sun will shine in our lives. For believers, the sun rises again and again, regardless of the circumstances. We may fall down a thousand times, but we get back up yet again. Proverbs 24:16 "for though the righteous fall seven times, they rise again, but the wicked stumble when calamity strikes". Our faith in God, His word is our only strength and hope.

CHAPTER X

J. FAITH IN THE FACE OF ADVERSITY AND TERROR

Where is faith when terror strikes? Beginning with September 11, 2001 the World Trade Center, thinking about what occurred at Sandy Hook Elementary massacre in December 14, 2012 in Connecticut. Fast forward all the way to Great Britain in May 22, 2017 we could all put a face to hatred and violence. While we are not used to these types of subhuman acts, we are continuously regurgitating the same questions, but no new answers have surfaced. In the face of terror, everyone from all walks of life and religious faiths come together to support victims and families affected by mass terror and violence. Unfortunately, months later following such heinous crimes, everyone goes about their everyday lives. When we do not forget, we also realized life goes on, and in fact, it does. Until the next tragedy strikes, we live in fear of the unknown notwithstanding continuous efforts and promises on the parts of politicians, global lawmakers, and church leaders to put an end to violence.

This pattern of joining, gathering, and temporary collaboration between various denominations and religious affiliations seems to have finally run its course. This interfaith collaboration has become a way of coping for the critical mass. We meet to pray collectively, we cry together, and we promise to do better until the news blows over, and we find ourselves too busy to take a bite out of sheer insanity. We know that "consequently, faith comes from hearing the message, and the message is heard through the Word of Christ" (Romans 10:17). The faith that comes by hearing is not necessarily the faith that a nation in mourning is expected to display. The faith that sustains long after the fear is gone can only come from a supernatural source God. But what we fail to understand is the simple fact that God is real.

God has feelings. He sympathizes with our suffering and pain. After all, "He was pierced for our transgressions, he was crushed for our iniquities, the punishment that brought us peace was on him, and by his wounds, we are healed" (Isaiah 53:5). Today, in the face of tribulations and great pain, we see a demonstration of superficial or temporary faith rather than true faith that is rooted in the knowledge of God and the application of His Word. What happened in Orlando, Florida, on June 12, 2016 is simply a reminder that fear is real, and we can see fear in action.

Faith keeps us going long after the fear dissipates and long after the causal factors are gone or dealt with. To speak about faith without fear would be a disservice to those who keep faith alive during great tragedy and terror. In an article from the *Boston Globe* entitled, "Voice out Gun Apologist," Adrian Walker wrote: "There will always be a path to create fear" (Walker, 2016). While this may be true, we must not cheapen the power to stand alone, if need be, to lend a hand to those whose lives have been disrupted by violence and the threat of violence. It is often said that talk is cheap, and that action speak louder than words. However, in the face of such terror, one can be so overwhelmed with grief and fear that action seems impossible. Walker Adrian went on to write: "in responding to terror specifically domestic terror is that mass shootings are not uncommon in this country, and the motivation vary" (Walker, 2016). The negative side to this is that "tragedy always seems to be followed by pledges to come together" (Walker, 2016).

This article delves into some interesting facts and ideology regarding terror and the responsibility of all citizens. Faith that conquers fear must be deeply rooted in genuine love and caring for all people irrespective of their gender, sexual preferences, creed, ethnicity, class, or religious affiliation. Unity must be a way of life, not a temporary show of support for all from all only when terror strikes. The expression "Fake it till you make it" does not apply when the stakes are too high.

Great Britain has not been exempted from the carnage and indescribable acts of terror that have been happening all over the world. Again, on March 22, 2017, a fifty-two-year-old man drove on the Westminster Bridge and killed at least six people including himself. Forty-nine were injured. About one month later, on May 22, another cruel act of evil took place. Someone chose to end the lives of young children at Manchester Arena with a bomb that took the lives of twenty people and wounded at least one hundred and twenty people. On June 3rd, at least three different episodes of criminal and heartbreaking scenarios took place.

For those families, the nation, those lives will never be the same again. The spirit and the determination of the people of London showed in the face of adversity is what conviction can do. As opposed to being afraid and intimidated, the public chose faith. They commonly agreed to come together to believe that evil is temporary, but love and faith are permanent, and they endure it all.

To face fear in the eye and declared they will not be intimidated. To stand on their desire to support those families affected by those tragedies, on Sunday, June 4, 2017, the nation reunited as one, and they organized an eventful concert. That concert benefitted those young survivors and those who lost their loved ones. More importantly, they agreed to look evil in the eye and to say, "I am not afraid of you, and I will live the life that has been given to me because it is a blessing." What about us, believers in Christ? It is about time for us to understand the value of a life and what a soul is worth and to stand for what is right? Fear should not be the bridge to reach your full potential and to catch on the purposeful life that God has for us. We must stand in love and charity, and we ought to continue believing that love is stronger than hate. Because of

His compassion, unconditional love God sent His only Son who agreed to die for us.

The lives of the next generation deserve to express the real manifestation of love. This is not worth faking, and the lives of our children and those who are reaching out for help, are worth far more than just an empty promise without action. Why risk another act of violence and hatred? As the saying goes, "To do it tomorrow, you have to plan it today." Life is real. Life is those highs and those lows but more importantly, life is us! We must act and declare authority over any negative thoughts of wickedness or incarceration. Faith is the language, a way of living and thinking. Faith is a vision but also, knowledge. Faith is unity and a legacy that is worth passing along.

Each home and family should start treating one another with respect, love, kindness, and compassion, we can start a movement of unconditional love that will transcend and make a better society. Our nation needs to be reminded of the command to "Love one another. As I have loved you, so you must love one another. By this everyone will know that you are my disciples if you love one another" (John 13:34). As we go back to the Word of God and continue to seek His presence, we will be able to not only care and love others as we want to be loved and be treated. We will reach a point where we understand that the greatest love of all is the sacrifice on the cross. Therefore, the only thing left to do is to act upon it. "If anyone, then, knows the good they ought to do and doesn't do it, it is sin for them" (James 4:17).

You are no longer an orphan. Regardless of what happened in the past, the lack of love you experienced when you thought you needed it the most. Hatred does not have to dominate over you. You may feel betrayed by someone you knew and feeling hurt emotionally and physically. Maybe the person you loved and needed the most is the one who took away your innocence, pride, and dreams. Do not worry, there is still life in you. The breath of God is in you, so you can reverse the hate to love. You can experience an unconditional love that you have never experienced before, should you agree to surrender and to believe in the peace that God can give you.

Finding and experiencing that love is no easy task. Especially when everyone around you is all about hate, judgment and hypocrisy. One thing that I know for sure is that the person who is calling you this time is exceptional. Please try the encounter with this man, Jesus Christ. Only a meeting with our heavenly father can make you whole again. If we stand in the Word of God, agree to hold on to His promises, we will keep on believing because this too shall pass. "Heaven and earth will pass away, but my Words will never pass away" (Matthew 24:35). Challenges and fears are all around us, as well as the opportunity to hold on to faith and believing. "Who is it that overcomes the world? Only the one who believes that Jesus is the Son of God." (1 John 5:5), in Him we have power and authority, and His glory should be revealed in due time.

1. Faith in the Twenty-First Century

With increased and constant violence in the news, people are discouraged, scared, and withdrawn at times. One cannot turn on the television, search the Internet, or read the local paper without being bombarded with mass shooting, abuse, neglect, or mistreatment. Some of the key events are cited to make into perspective where faith lies in the mist of carnage in this Twenty first Century.

Who can ever forget some of those insane acts of violence when a gunman entered Marjory Stoneman Douglas, a Florida High School on February 15, 2018, and murdered 17 people within 10 minutes? After killing those many people, the gunman who was a former student, had the audacity to walk out undetected leaving the scene in a crowd of students. Even though he was later apprehended; those 17 lives are departed, and the lives of the family members are incessantly changed.

At Mandalay Bay Resort in Las Vegas on October 2, 2017 an additional massacre took place. 58 killed and 500 injured when a shooter opened fire on the crowd of concert-goers at a country music festival. People left their home and families with the hope of having fun and that entertainment turned into destruction and despair.

The fury continues: On June 12, 2016, a gunman entered a nightclub in Orlando and shot forty-nine young people who were there to have a great time. The number of dead bodies increases with each massacre. Regardless where you live or what you do it seems tragedy, anguish and hopelessness become the order of the day for any town or city. A gunman opened fire during a Sunday service at the First Baptist Church in Sutherland Springs, a little town in Wilson County. 26 people have been killed and 20 injured on November 2017.

In San Bernardino, California in December 2015, a newlywed couple took the lives of 14 people and injured 22 others when they stormed in an office party at a social service center.

On December 14, 2012, a Friday like any other Friday, parents and school bus drivers drove students to Sandy Hook Elementary. The teachers and all the staff were ready to have another great day in the school specifically the last day before the weekend. None of them knew it would be the end of their journey on earth. Without any form of mercy or any sense of compassion, a gunman, prior to leave his home, killed and shot his mother, then entered the elementary school in Connecticut and killed at least twenty children and six adults. That was evil at its worst. The world stood still in utter shock and disbelief, which were soon transformed into anger and rage. Same old stories, so we must get rid of guns one would say. Well, we know that getting rid of guns is not the solution rather a band aid for the human heart and soul. "My people perish for lack of knowledge" (Hosea 6:4).

One may ask what knowledge the apostle is writing about. Well, we know that the Word of God has the power to transform and to renew all who are lost and heavy laden. "God so loved the world that He gave his only begotten son so that whosoever believe in him shall not perish but have everlasting life" (John 3:16). Now then, we may ask ourselves this: If this verse is true, why so much violence and so little love and care from this so call Savior? So many are perishing daily, Violence continues to increase at a steady pace with no end in sight. Regardless of all the protest about guns, laws and regulations this generation seems to be losing faith, hope and the good life they were told they will enjoy. Many people question if this propaganda about God is real? While those who are still holding on to faith in God start doubting and wondering.

After September 11, 2001, when the Twin Towers of the World Trade Center and the Top Military Building in the Capital of Washington; the Pentagon were attacked, America increased homeland security and attempted to secure our borders, but still the violence continues. From Boston and Chicago to New York City, gang violence has no boundaries.

From little boys, as young as five years of age in the street and elementary-school students in their classroom to young adults in the nightclub, death reaches anyone in the America. The thought of eradicating violence altogether is a dream that every parent dream of constantly, especially parents of African American children. Today the conversation is still the same and little progress to none has been done to eradicate the number of innocent lives that could have been saved.

Faith is a process throughout various experiences in life. From one massacre to another, most of us still have a reason to smile and to stand firm because God pulls most of us through. He takes away all our fears, uncertainties, and doubts. Furthermore, He erases our scars, He makes us new, and He renews our spirits with hope, life and desire to make a difference in people's lives. We no longer have to be victims; we can be survivors and prayer warriors who have found a river of living waters. Regardless of what the enemy tries to throw at us, we will come out victorious without a trace of anger. "And if Christ has not been raised, your faith is futile; you are still in your sins" (1 Corinthians 1:17).

Who are we to talk about faith when we are just sinners? Who are we to even stand here and still be in our right minds when the enemy's plan was to destroy us, yet again we are still standing in God's promise and will for our lives? The enemy does have some power to see how God has created us for great things so that we can make a difference in some people's lives. Hence, he comes to destroy that seed in us. Today our testimony is that our seed will grow, we will live to inspire and to become a true servant of the Lord. The Word of God reminds us "It shall come to pass afterward that I will pour out My Spirit upon all flesh; and your sons and your daughters shall prophesy, your old men shall dream dreams, your young men shall see visions" (Joel 2: 28).

In this era, even though we have seen, suffered, and heard how the enemy is trying to pull us from our goals, we also have seen miracles in the lives of our children and family members. "That our sons may be as plants grown up in their youth; that our daughters may be as pillars" (Psalm 144:12). A young boy was playing sport for his school, but he fell during the game and since that day was paralyzed. His parents, church, and the community prayed and never stop praying when most of the best specialists lost hope to see him walk again. When he was no longer going to therapy, while at home, God revealed Himself to him, and he started to walk on his own. Amazing miracles are still happening in our times in the lives of our youth. 1 Timothy 4:12 says "Don't let anyone look down on you because you are young, but set an example for the believers in speech, in conduct, in love, in faith and in purity".

In this twenty-first century, more than ever we cannot let what we see and hear in the news determine our paths. God is using our sons and daughters, our youth. We need to be in a place to understand the level of authority that we all have. "The tongue has the power of life and death, and those who love it will eat its fruit" (Proverbs 18: 21). How could the same mouth that says, "We believe" also say "We are afraid"? Must one of them be dominant? If fears are the dominant forces in your life, it is time to go to the other side. By God's grace you can get there. Educators; teach, leaders; lead, preachers; preach, prayer warriors; pray, dreamers; dream. Fear is only an annoying disturbance.

CHAPTER XI
K. WAYS TO CULTIVATE FAITH IN GOD

1. Faith in Our Day-to-Day Life

Studies have shown how a lot of people suffer from headaches or malaise. Therefore, doctors offer them some medicine to alleviate the pain. Most of those patients follow through and take the medicine with the hope that they will get better; some do get some relief and others none. By taking medicine alone, we display a great amount of faith. Hope that by following orders, we will feel restored. Hence, we experience faith daily. For example, an expecting mother exercises faith while fixing the room of her unborn child, nevertheless, none of us know what life entails; however, we plan daily as if we had full control of what is to come. At times, you may think that God does not respond to your prayers, but His answers come in many forms because he says, "For my thoughts are not your thoughts neither are your ways my ways, declares the LORD" (Isaiah 59:8-9). He knows our needs and wants, and his plan for us is certain. It is a matter of believing without seeing, which we are doing daily but fail to execute it when it matters the most in our Christian lives.

To truly access the level of faith that can transcend the mind, first and for most we should totally surrender ourselves to God. We should also let God take control of things that we will never have control over. As well as remaining in an attitude of belief that sooner than later, God will guide us through. In the book of Psalms 37:5, David stated, "I was young and now I am old, yet I have never seen the righteous forsaken or their children begging bread." As believers, depending on the Lord on our day-to-day activities has a lot to do with total submission when our reality is unbearable. When children are acting out, our country is in war against one another, or when a husband decides to leave, when there is no food or shelter, we must lift our eyes up to the mountains because "My help comes from the Lord, the Maker of heaven and earth" (Psalm 121:2).

Reaching that point of submission is holding on to hope and faith. It is an example of truly believing that regardless of what is going on in our lives, "The righteous person may have many troubles, but the Lord delivers him from them all; he protects all his bones, not one of them will be broken" (Psalm 34:19-20). In our routine, we will fall but we will get back up again. The books of Proverbs put it this way: "For though the righteous fall seven times, they rise again, but the wicked stumble when calamity strikes" (Proverbs 24:16).

We have been given the Word of God and we fall short in using it for our own good. There is nothing that is going on in our lives that is new to God; He is the beginning and the end, and He knows what we are dealing with in our lives. We need to act with wisdom and understand what Paul reminded us in the book of Ephesians: "For our struggle is not against flesh and blood, but against the rulers, against the authorities, against the powers of this dark world and against the spiritual forces of evil in the heavenly realms." Hence, let us arm ourselves with the armor of God, "stand firm then, with the belt of truth buckled around your waist, with the breastplate of righteousness in place, and with your feet fitted with the readiness that comes from the gospel of peace. In addition to all this, take up the shield of faith, with which you can extinguish all the flaming arrows of the evil one. Take the helmet of salvation and the sword of the Spirit, which is the Word of God" (Ephesians 6:12-17).

When we master those skills, we understand the power of those armors that have been given to us. Too often we have failed to use them properly when trials and tribulations come our way.

2. Stop, and count God's Blessings in Your Life.

You woke up this morning; regardless of what happened last night, you are here. You have been given a clean sheet to write whatever you want to write and an opportunity to do whatever you need to do today.

Take a moment and realize that you are breathing. That is your blessing. Consequently, let us start counting our blessings. There will always be some people who are more fortunate than us. Our attitude towards life determines who we have chosen to be or where we want to go. The famous Zig Ziglar (2009) stated, "Your attitude, not your aptitude, will determine your altitude."

When life decides to throw challenges from left to right, we need strength and hope. Let us remember, "The joy of the Lord is our strength" (Nehemiah 8:10). Because of God's grace and mercy, we are no longer adulterers or liars. We are not special or more spiritual than anyone, but when we live in His presence and allow Him to dominate over our desires, lust, and thoughts. We can reach and taste the power of His sovereignty. We are renewed daily and challenged at times. However, being in a unique and intimate moment and relationship with God, we can remember what He has done and what He can still operate in our lives. He alone deserves all the glory and the honor. We should train our minds to count His blessings in our lives. What our hearts desire, crave, and hope for when things seem out of order is to recall that He has made a way for others and he can still make a way for us today. "Behold, I will do a new thing, now it shall spring forth; shall you not know it? I will even make a road in the wilderness and rivers in the desert" (Isaiah 45:19). Let us keep up the faith. Let us stay strong in the Lord our Savior, who said: "Be strong and of good courage, do not fear nor be afraid of them; for the LORD your God, He is the One who goes with you. He will not leave you nor forsake you" (Deuteronomy 31:6).

3. Remembering His Unconditional Love

Love drives most of us to do the unthinkable. When we are in love, we tend to forget time, space, and sometimes ourselves, so the other person can pay attention and acknowledge us. But the greatest love of all is a gift for our salvation. That gift was given to us, so we can start over and fulfill our purpose because "There is no fear in love; but perfect love casts out fear: because fear hath torment. He that fear is not made perfect in love. We love him because he first loved us" (1 John 4:18-19).

As we rely on God's promise, we can reach a maturity of total surrender. According to Dr. Youssef, "There is no doubt that fear is a very powerful emotion, but what matters most is how we deal with it. In every moment of fear, we encounter, God is giving us an opportunity to check our spiritual temperature to gauge our fuel tank of faith and to check the status of our walk with Him" (p. 2). To love and to know how to love, we need to experience love. God showed us His unrestricted love when He became flesh. "For a child will be born to us, a son will be given to us; And the government will rest on His shoulders; And His name will be called Wonderful Counselor, Mighty God, Eternal Father, Prince of Peace" (Isaiah 9:6). There is no one else who could love as God. "He who does not love does not know God, for God is love" (1 John 4:8).

CHAPTER XII

L. THE PRESENCE OF THE LORD, THE HOLY SPIRIT

In addition to faith and total dependence on God, one must seek His presence with the expectation that He will come through no matter what the time, the circumstances, or the difficulty. In God's presence, we can always expect the unexpected. "I will call upon the Lord, who is worthy to be praised; so, shall I be saved from my enemies. When the waves of death surrounded me, the floods of ungodliness made me afraid…the snares of death confronted me. In my distress, I called upon the Lord, and cried out to my God; He heard my voice from His temple, and my cry entered His ears" (2 Samuel 22:4-7).

Each one of us delights in the Word and His holy presence differently. Joyce Meyer (1996) reminded us of the following: "You are an individual, and God has an individual plan for you that will be manifested if you will continue to seek Him for it" (pp. 77-78). Having an intimate and personal relationship with God is the best and only way to experience faith. However, with everything that is going on around the world fear, natural diseases, war, despair, darkness, and insanity can people truly have faith? The Word of God tells us, "Do not love the world or anything in the world. If anyone loves the world, love for the Father is not in them." For everything in the world, the lust of the flesh, the lust of the eyes, and the pride of life comes not from the Father but from the world" (1 John 2:15-16).

God Himself, who created the world, nonetheless, is telling us to be cautious. That alone is an instruction that authorizes us to not live instinctively. Lives are transformed, regenerated when the Holy Spirit is active in us. God loves us so much that He gave His only son to die on the cross for sins that He did not commit. Therefore, for this unselfish act alone, it is worthwhile to take the time to reevaluate His love. Hence, relying on His Word and His Spirit is the only way we can find clarity and hope. This distorted world can only cause fears that would hinder us from realizing God's destiny and plan for us and for future generations. Through the Word, by keeping we centered and accountable, we can define and make a difference in our lives and those around us. According to Meyer (1996), "There are certain individuals to whom God gives the gift of faith for specific occasions such as a dangerous missionary trip or a very challenging situation, when this gift is operating in people they are able to comfortably believe God for something that other people would see as impossible" (p. 101). The disciples had to wait for that advocate; the Holy Spirit before heading to the world and preach the Gospel.

Brutus Betina, from a prayer group named "Seekers voice" defines the acronym PUSH as "Pray Until Something Happens" and from personal experience, most of us have learned that "Because with God's Word we will gain the victory that He provides. We will trample down our enemies" (Psalm 60:12). Therefore, it is through commitment, total surrender and by letting the Holy Spirit command our path in faith that we can see God's will revealed in our lives and nations.

1. The Word of God

How important is the Word of God, what does it really mean to us? In one of his Psalms, David declared: "Your Word is a lamp to guide me and a light for my path" (Psalm 119:105). In this world of darkness, where would we be without the Word of God? The Bible is one of the best tools any believer cannot afford to live without. All of us can access it, however, it is yet to be determined why many of us do not use such a powerful weapon that encourages us and gives us hope when this hope is in such a short supply.

Unfortunately, we do not read or meditate in the Word of God as often as we should. Many of us have a Bible in the living room for others to see, but we forget to use it to feed our soul and spirit. "All Scripture is given by inspiration of God, and is profitable for doctrine, for reproof, for correction, for instruction in righteousness, that the man of God may be complete, thoroughly equipped for every good work" (2 Timothy 3:16-17). The knowledge and depth of wisdom that we can gather from our Bible with the Holy Spirit's guidance is a direct connection, the key and the power of knowing Jesus at a higher level. This knowledge is not from the world; it is classified information for the elect ones. It also a contribution to the highest level of spiritual growth, as well as a wealth of learning. The Word of God is water to our thirst of understanding; it is an empowering tool in times of trials.

The Word of God inspires, transforms, and transcends people's lives. The Word of God is rich with authority and dominion. "He who believes in me, as the Scripture has said, out of his heart will flow rivers of living water" (John 7:38). The Word of God is food that we cannot afford to live without. It is our source for salvation and that salvation is only received through faith. The Word of God is life itself a testimony of the foundation of the world and God's revelation of what's to come. "The grass withers and the flowers fall, but the Word of our God endures forever" (Isaiah 40:8). If you are seeking wisdom and superior knowledge, the Bible is the source of it all. The things of the world may seem the best to have; however, the finest is always in God. In Him, we have it all to win and nothing to lose. Our lack of faith hinders us from believing the authority and power there is in the name of Jesus and His Word. If only we were to take the Word of God as our compass, we will always be in the right path where we belong, in His promise.

2. If We Only Knew

It is in our DNA to be strong, to be prosperous to live the abundant life that He provides, and to be victorious. More often we forget whose we are and what we are made of; we are children of God, Genesis 1:27 remind us "God created man in His own image, in the image of God He created him; male and female He created them. Therefore, when we agree to walk with God, to follow His Word, and to live by faith we declare that we are free. "... you are no longer a slave, but a son; and if a son, then an heir through God" (Galatians 4:7).

Calamities, destruction and horror may create a sense of hopelessness in our day to day life but more than ever, we need to embrace what is true and certain, the Word. "Then the Spirit of the LORD came on Jahaziel son of Zechariah, the son of Benaiah, the son of Jeiel, the son of Mattaniah, a Levite and descendant of Asaph, as he stood in the assembly. He said: 'Listen, King Jehoshaphat and all who live in Judah and Jerusalem! This is what the LORD says to you: Do not be afraid or discouraged because of this vast army. For the battle is not yours, but God's" (2 Chronicles 20:14-15). This message is also our message in this day and age; all the madness can still be going on around us, disease, violence, pain, war, and fear, but we will succeed, our children will live and they will be prosperous because "With God we will gain the victory," (Psalm 60:12) and "then our sons in their youth will be like well-nurtured plants, and our daughters will be like pillars carved to adorn a palace" (Psalm 114:12).

Job, one of the most courageous and faithful men of the Bible, was tested by the vicissitudes of life. When Satan dared Jesus to test him, Job's faith somehow increased due to the profound connection and intimate relationship he had with God. Job knew who God was and he remained faithful. It was imperative for him to encourage himself and to trust in God no matter what. This is the perfect relationship.

He knew God at a level that most of us need to reach. It was a sincere relationship. He believed in God when all seemed lost and falling apart, and God knew his heart. It is the same scenario for us; we ought to team up with God. By teaming up with God, we learn to testify and to acknowledge that there are good benefits in having a relationship with Him.

We will never fail if we choose God and decide to team up with Him. God is not unjust, contrary to popular belief. God believes in us. He knows that we may be weak, yet most importantly, He counts on us and He has our backs what an insurance! "For I know the plans I have for you," declares the LORD, "plans to prosper you and not to harm you, plans to give you hope and a future. Then you will call on me and come and pray to me, and I will listen to you" (Jeremiah 29:11-12). Those Words are not from flesh and blood; they come directly from our Savior and redeemer. Hence, *"When Jesus says yes, nobody can say no"* (Michelle Williams,2014). Because God says it, that settles it! The message of Jesus Christ is in His Word.

3. God Made a Way Where There Was No Way

There are many women who have been told they will not be able to carry a child. After countless visits to the doctors, many tryouts, and spending so much money, they came to accept that there would be no hope of bearing a child. However, when you have a promise from the Highest, all things are possible. We have had the opportunity to listen to many couples that were married for over twenty years, and they had not been able to become pregnant. Through prayers and keeping up the faith on a Word they had received from God, they were blessed with a child without a surrogate or assistance from the medical field. "Let us hold fast the confession of our hope without wavering, for He who promised is faithful" (Hebrews 10:23). The same God, who gives understanding and knowledge to some doctors, had a better plan for these couples. Hence, as humans, when our strength and ability is limited, God's power is limitless. We came to terms with the understanding that the Word "impossible" is nowhere to be found when it comes to God. There is simply power in the name of Jesus. "For the vision is yet for an appointed time; but at the end it will speak, and it will not lie. Though it tarries, wait for it; because it will surely come, it will not tarry" (Habakkuk 2:3).

The people of Israel did not know where to go when the armies of Egypt were after them. God opened the red sea used a pillar of cloud at night that brought darkness to the one side and light to the other side. He delivered them from the Egyptians (Exodus 14). Our God is the same God; never changing. Regardless of the highs or the lows, the good and the bad; the unknown and the known, the battles or the fear, He is the source of it all. He can, and He will continue to make a way where there is no way because He is the Way, the Light and the Truth.

CHAPTER XIII
M. FAITH CAN PULL YOU THROUGH

In these circumstances where hope and belief seem like an old distant song. By making a firm decision and total commitment it is granted that faith can pull you through. The best is yet to come in your life. In addition to faith, one must seek His presence with the expectation that He will come through no matter what the time, the circumstances, or the difficulty may be. In His presence, you can always expect the unexpected. The only mechanism we must use is to speak the Word, to call on Him, to pray and He will be there if we believe. "You will seek me and find me when you seek me with all your heart" (Jeremiah 29:13). Faith can only be experienced by having an intimate and personal relationship with God.

How many times do we go to the source, we remember our Creator and Savior, when all seems overwhelming? What used to be right is wrong and what is wrong is right. We depend on our feelings and we forget that feelings can change from one moment to another. In this life, we must choose compassion over hate. The power of the Word keeps us centered, accountable, we can define and make a difference in our lives and those around us. We have a mission and a message for the world. By battling fears, doubts, worries, and uncertainties, we can gain strength, anointing, revelation and as well as faith. Faith needs to be experienced daily, it is one of the challenges for believers who are unable to grasp the idea that God has full control over our lives. Fear is a liar that some of us have not catch up yet, today we know that we have been manipulated and blindfolded. Fear is a thief that has been stealing your crops and makes you believe, it is a lack of rain or drought. Consequently, it is time to wake up and stand firm in faith that you are free, because the truth set us free, we are no longer slaves of lies and deceitfulness. "Then you will know the truth, and the truth will set you free" (John 8: 32).

Now that we can perceive and discover the mystery of those lies, we must stand firm and refocus on the Word, the Truth, the Light and the only Way who is Jesus Christ. Having only faith in the name of Jesus Christ and total awakening can defend and pull us through the claws of depression and insecurity. We will rise and speak truth and life to our circumstances because we have unveiled the hidden empty and false accusation of fear. Through reading and staying in the word daily the infusion of strength and undying hope enables us to stand firm again.

From the album Chain Breaker, Zach Williams' lyrics depict the negativity and mendacities about fear in his song titled: Fear Is a Liar. *"When he told you you're not good enough. When he told you you're not right. When he told you you're not strong enough to put up a good fight. When he told you you're not worthy? When he told you you're not loved. When he told you you're not beautiful. Fear, he is a liar He will take your breath Stop you in your steps Fear he is a liar He will rob your rest Steal your happiness Cast your fear in the fire"* ...

How many of us have felt inadequate, unworthy or undeserving of a life that God let our path? Today, recognize the true characteristics of the enemy who is ready to steal your life, your happiness, your children and most of all, the destiny that God has for you.

1. He Gave Us Power through His Compassion

Nothing is final until God said it is. When you have a relationship with Him, daily you experience different levels of hope and transformation. As He keeps you closer, you can reach a new dimension, a new revelation, a new gift and a new anointing. His presence takes away our fears and makes us whole again. Being born in a family or region doesn't have to mean that your life has no purpose, or you must accept to live in misery and distress always. God encourages us to come to Him in prayer, as he told us to "pray continually" (1 Thessalonians 5:17). As we pray we need to be vigilant daily. "Be always on the watch and pray that you may be able to escape all that is about to happen and that you may be able to stand before the Son of Man" (Luke 21:36).

Jabez was vigilant, he chose to go to God and to ask Him to transform his life. Our life does not have to be determined by the world or even by our parents, but through prayer we are able to act with authority and power and not settle for less than the best. "Jabez cried out to the God of Israel, 'Oh that you would bless me and enlarge my territory! Let your hand be with me and keep me from harm so that I will be free from pain.' And God granted his request" (1 Chronicles 4:10). He declared that pain would not dominate over his life, and Jabez asked for a favor.

In return, we can follow Jabez's example as we teach our children to seek God in prayer. In His unconditional love and mercy, God gave Jabez what his heart desired and He can still do the same for us. Samson refused to die without a last victory even though he did not follow God's instruction. God showed his compassion toward Samson. People cannot determine what your life will be. Balaam was unable to curse the people who God already blessed. "How can I curse those whom God has not cursed? How can I denounce those whom the Lord has not denounced?" (Numbers 23:8), this passage alone tells us that at this difficult time in our lives; the struggle that you are going through right now is not permanent. This situation is temporary, and we are going through it with success. Yes, we are going through because it is not that destiny that the Lord has promised. Hence, let us remind ourselves that we are the chosen ones. We are in this moment, in this situation, in this location for a reason; just endure it all so you can build character. You are here because God has a plan for your life. Let us keep our eyes on Him; He is never late, even though it may feel like it. In just another moment, we will roar, we will soar high as an eagle because you were created to fly and not to walk with our heads down. Today we are going to do something that we have not done before, we are going to believe that in Him, and through Him we can. "With God, we will gain the victory, and he will trample down our enemies" (Psalm 108:13).

2. Building a Relationship with God in Prayer

When we love someone, it is a natural response to spend time with that person. As we spend time talking, learning and discovering who this person is, we start knowing that person better and we start building a stronger feeling and relationship. This reality is also true when we come to the Lord in prayer. At times, we do not have to say anything, just to be present and to be available to Him and we can feel His presence and anointing upon us. "Likewise, the Spirit also helps in our weaknesses. For we do not know what we should pray for as we ought, but the Spirit Himself makes intercession for us with groaning which cannot be uttered" (Romans 8:26).

For this to be true, we need to be available, patient, obedient and hopeful to encounter God. Hence, our prayer is the ability to communicate with our Father and Savior with Words, songs, and dances. It is also a way for Him to connect with us as our souls and spirits reach the point of the most intense dialogue. Yes, prayer is not one-way connection, God is also speaking. Prayer is a conversation and the most intimate one we can ever have with our counselor, our Father and provider. In many ways, prayer helps us to conquer our fears, so prayers cannot just be, "Jesus, here I am" or "God, you know." We must have an intimate relationship with God to feel His presence and to go to Him in prayer. Henceforth, it is necessary to pray for our faith to grow in God for it is said,

"Because you have so little faith. Truly I tell you, if you have faith as small as a mustard seed, you can say to this mountain, 'Move from here to there,' and it will move. Nothing will be impossible for you" (Matthew 17:20). One would think that we could easily tell the fear to disappear from our lives, but we know better. We know it takes hard work and commitment to deal with any problem, fear is no different.

Building a relationship with God is a process that started on the cross, when Jesus agreed to give His life for us. Therefore, let us be present, let us be open, and let us be mindful of the knowledge and opportunity to seek His presence. Building a relationship with someone who already knows who you are and already loves you is humbling. Regardless of who you are, where you come from, or what you have done, you can always redeem that unconditional relationship. Most of us fail to pray because we claim that we do not know how to pray. I have good news for you: you do not need to know how to pray. What you need is an open heart and total surrender and you will see how His hand will guide you. His blood will cover you, and you will never be the same again. If you need a relationship, and you have the desire to connect with someone, Jesus is the One. He would not judge or condemn you, but He will guide you to the right path. He will open your eyes and install His Holy Spirit within you. As you let go and allow Him to take over your life, in His presence you will want to stay because it is the best time you will ever experience in your entire life.

3. Faith in Relation to Prayer

According to Abigail Rian Evans, "Our prayer cannot make God give us more or deepen God's desire for our health, but they reflect thanksgiving for God's goodness and love for us" (Evans, 1998). At times people pray repetitively as though they can force the hand of God or cause Him to do exactly what they want at a time. I often hear people praying out loud in church asking God to "give me victory, and I will give you praise." This type of bargaining is ludicrous and sounds bad to those who listen in. "Prayer shows our dependence upon God" (Ibid p. 76). We have been saved for God's purpose, and all he requires is for us to trust and obey. Any time we feel that there is something that we can do so God can do more for us, we fail to follow his Word "With God all things are possible" (Ibid.). Other people who may be sick tend to substitute medicine for prayer believing that prayer is not the solution, but prescribed medicine is. We know for sure that the Word of God is powerful and "Therefore confess your sins to each other and pray for each other so that you may be healed. The prayer of a righteous person is powerful and effective" (James 5:16). The problem is the ways and means of being righteous may not be clear to some people. In the case of a sick person, "prayer is efficacious even if the disease continues to run its course" (Ibid., p. 77).

Prayer is important for many reasons. It is a way to calm the troubled spirit. Moreover, it provides a safety net from the possible danger, which almost always comes because of not knowing the outcome at times. "Even if the body is not cured, the soul is restored" (Ibid.). Although the goal of every prayer is a solution to a problem, our resolve must be to glorify God no matter what the outcome may be. "Jesus is our tutor and examples in all things, and nowhere is that clearer than in our prayer" (Dr. David Jeremiah, p. 11). More than ever, we must be knowledgeable if we are to be prayer warriors. Apostle John teaches us that "in the beginning was the Word, the Word was with God, and the Word was God" (John 1:1). To know God, we must know his Word. Thus, knowledge is power. We cannot pray if we do not know God, "A failure of prayer in our life is generally a failure to know Jesus" (Ibid, p. 12). Learning how to pray is essential to our overall sense of well-being. We cannot be effective at what we do not know, yet we attempt to pray without first learning how to. The author writes what many may feel or experience: "I learn how to pray out of desperation" (Ibid, p.11).

A funny thing happens when we find ourselves in a situation when we must pray; then we are forced to practice a skill that we have no prior knowledge of. Prayer is to our soul what oxygen is to our body. We simply cannot make it without prayer. While we should not wait until problems arise to pray, most often "we pray because we are without any other recourse" (Ibid.). Like children, we run to our earthly father when we are anxious or upset. God expects the same, but he requires trust, obedience, and nearness for He says, "Come near to God and he will come near to you. Wash your hands, you sinners, and purify your hearts, you double-minded" (James 4:8). This promise is certain as we seek to navigate through life with all the trials and tribulations that are sure to come our way.

Prayer is an example of believing that you are not alone and that you have the one who is "worthy to take the scroll and to open its seals because you were slain...and they will reign on the earth" (Revelation 5:9 - 10). Prayer is reaching, touching, and feeling the presence of God in deep connection, with the give and take of harmonious conversation. Prayer is a dedication of sacred time with the Highest that is led by the Holy Spirit. Prayer is one of the unique and special ways to communicate with our Father. During His journey on earth, Jesus taught His disciples how to pray. "Our Father in heaven hallowed be your name...And lead us not into temptation but deliver us from the evil one" (Matthew 6:9-13). This is insurance that we are not alone. We are not fatherless, we have a role model in our lives and we have a provider and a teacher who is ready and willing to take over if only we let Him. He created us with free will. Prayer is praising God for his compassion, love, and faithfulness. Prayer is a confession from our wrongdoings; it is making petitions, intercessions, thankfulness, and supplication.

Prayer is light and strength when adversity strikes. The prayer of a believer has no limitation and it ignores space and time. In Acts 12: 6-10 it recalls the story of Peter who was freed from prison and how the supernatural materialized. "When Herod was about to bring him out, that night Peter was sleeping, bound with two chains between two soldiers; and the guards before the door were keeping the prison. Now behold, an angel of the Lord stood by him, and a light shone in the prison; and he struck Peter on the side and raised him up, saying, "Arise quickly!" And his chains fell off his hands. Then the angel said to him, "Gird yourself and tie on your sandals"; and so, he did. And he said to him, "Put on your garment and follow me." So, he went out and followed him, and did not know that what was done by the angel was real, but thought he was seeing a vision. When they were past the first and the second guard posts, they came to the Iron Gate that leads to the city, which opened to them of its own accord; and they went out and went down one street, and immediately the angel departed from him". That is what prayer and faith can still do in this time of urgency. That is a testimony of power, victory when faith is in action.

Prayer is for our soul like the rain is for the earth. Prayer is the symbol of faith for what is asked. Even if it's not seen, it will be granted. Dr. Caroline Leaf reported, "even though toxic thought can cause brain damage; prayer can reverse that damage and cause the brain and body to thrive." Now more than ever, we ought to be able to connect to the source and to bring all things to the Lord in prayer. Sometimes, it depends where we are, or what situation that we are facing, we can just pray in our hearts, using Words that the Holy Spirit is inspiring us as well as praising Him for who God is and all that He does in our lives. Prayer can be a song or even a deep breath that God can hear. It is astounding how the Holy Spirit has the power to transform and to express our exhalations into comprehensible prayers. Moreover, Dr. Leaf added, "There is growing interest in the power of prayer to change our brain and even matter itself. Even though as Christians we are cognizant of this by reading the Bible and from experience, it is nice to know science is now bearing this out."

While science continues to evolve, God's word is constant. Spending time in prayer may seem illogical but real for those who believe their strength comes from the source of all things. As powerful as prayer can be for those who believe, most of us are bound by an irrational fear that some of us would have never suffered from forty years ago; monophobia. Currently most of the people around the world may spend a day, a week even the whole year without praying or spending time in the Word. However, we are unable to stay a minute or a day without a phone. Essentially, monophobia according to psychology today *is the irrational fear of being without a working mobile phone or being unable to use your phone for some reason, such as the absence of a signal or running out of minutes or battery power.*

In the early 1920's, during the First World War the German tested wireless phones in military trains between Berlin and Zossen. Other countries such as Russia and United Kingdom followed along. Major development paved the way for the first cell phone. According to the Atlantic and other sources, it was in the late 1900's that the first cell phone was launched by a Motorola employee Martin Cooper who stood in midtown Manhattan and placed a call to the headquarters of Bell Labs in New Jersey. Priced at around 4,000 dollar we could only talk for about thirty minutes before dying; the model was a Motorola DynaTAC 800x. It was large sized, yet it was the most portable telephone ever made and for the first time in history, without constraints of wires or portable phone holders, a human being could call someone. It was the high end of technology at the time. It took us a long time to finally modify, refine and still working on how a phone should be.

100

However, for thousands of years, all of us have been introduced to a superior being who does not require a special connection, or the perfect sound wave to connect with us. If we had to wait for many years to connect with another person. Due to long or short distance, or physical presence; rest assured, having a connection with Jesus Christ right now does not have to cost you a penny or any technology. Some of us are still struggling on how to use the latest cell phone or any electronic devices. This special person only need your open heart and willingness to follow Him. He will guide, protect and love you as you never been loved or cherished and spoken before.

Whatever language you may speak, it does not matter where we come from, if we are fluent readers or not. It does not matter, if we have a terminal disease or all the awful things we have done in life. Through a sigh, or our last breath, we can call on His name. He can understand, listen and He is never too busy to ignore our call. As we call on the name of Jesus Christ, we will never be alone, we will never lose His signal because He lives inside of us!

4. Few of God's attributes

The One that has full authority on earth and in heaven gave us some commends, because He was able to follow command Himself. He knows the challenges and tests that we are facing daily, therefore when it was time to do the right thing, as difficult as things looked like, he agreed to give Himself for us. In Gethsemane, when Jesus realized it was time for Him to accomplished what he came on earth for. He shared "Watch and pray so that you will not fall into temptation. The spirit is willing, but the flesh is weak. ...He prayed, "My Father, if it is not possible for this cup to be taken away unless I drink it, may your will be done" (Matthew 26: 4-42).

It is not our will, the one who formed us in His own image knows our desires, our needs and He is the only One who can suffice to our thirst. Hence, we ought to know about the real characteristics and attributes about this Savior who told us to follow Him. Who is He really? We need to come to term why so many before us agreed to follow His command and to have faith in Him. Compare to what life has thrown at you lately, is it true there is someone who never change regardless of our mistakes? Yes, there is one, Jesus Christ of Nazareth!

God is Love

Love, isn't it what the world is craving for? "Whoever does not love does not know God, because God is love" 1 John 4: 8. Throughout the life of Jesus Christ, we have learned about His love for mankind and His life is imbedded with love. Without love, life is weak, filled with fear and despair. Love can comfort, accept all, forgive all over and over. Love is the manifestation and one of the greatest attributes of God. "And so, we know and rely on the love God has for us. God is love, whoever lives in love lives in God, and God in them" (1 John 4:16). The love of Jesus Christ is unconditional and has no limitation. It does not matter what we did or did not do. Regardless of your faults and wrong doing His love is everlasting. David was an adulterer, murderer, yet He called David "A Man after His Own Heart" (Acts 13: 22).

God is Immutable

From all God's attributes, this specific one shares how much He never changes. For many His immutability is one of the most comforting attributes of God. More often, our family members, parents or spouses change, but God revealed Him immutable through life. That alone, can be an attractive attribute that reminds us how much He cares and how much He is consistent through time and time. He is not God in our lives because we are obedient and following His command, He is God and He will never change despite our transgression. "I the Lord do not change. So you, the descendants of Jacob, are not destroyed." (Malachi 3:6). How much more we can confide in His Word for us? Who is like our God?

God is Self-Existent

God does not depend on anything for His continued existence. For as the Father hath life in himself; so hath he given to the Son to have life in himself" (John 5:26). We need the air to breathe; we need so much to maintain our life. At times, many of us argue what comes first, the chicken or the egg? With God, there is no hidden mystery of what comes first. God is Self-Existent; He does not rely on any machine or the air to function fully and powerfully. He is the beginning and the End. "Listen to Me, O Jacob, even Israel whom I called; I am He, I am the first, I am also the last" (Isaiah. 48:12).

God is Eternal

God transcends all time and temporal limitations and is thus infinite with respect to time. Everything in this life is temporary. The troubles, the headaches, the suffering and all that seems permanent in our lives will reach an end, but God and His word. "In the beginning was the Word, and the Word was with God, and the Word was God" (John 1:1).

Most of God 's attributes are beyond our knowledge and understanding; there are and will always be a mystery that goes beyond our imagination and satisfaction to our intellect.

God is Omniscient, Omnipresent, and Omnipotent. Who knows it all, that can do it all and manifest it all, but God. He knows about this book, about our lives and what is to come. He knows about the next horror and difficulty in our lives. From time to time we forget before, during and after in all that He remains God. "Before a word is on my tongue you, Lord, know it completely. You hem me in behind and before, and you lay your hand upon me. Such knowledge is too wonderful for me, too lofty for me to attain" (Psalms 139: 4-6).

God is omniscient, He is all knowing. His knowledge is perfect, full of wisdom and understanding, an absolute knowledge and nothing surprises God. He knows the present, the past and the future, "Oh, the depth of the riches and wisdom and knowledge of God! How unsearchable are his judgments and how inscrutable his ways"! Romans 11:33. He sees it all. "The eyes of the Lord are everywhere, keeping watch on the wicked and the good" (Proverbs15:3).

God is Omnipresent, He transcends it all. He is everywhere, in the mist of the storm, in your situation. There is no limitation when it comes to God. We cannot hide from our iniquities from Him. "Am I a God at hand, declares the Lord, and not a God afar off? Can a man hide himself in secret places so that I cannot see him? Declares the Lord, Do I not fill heaven and earth? Declares the Lord" (Jer. 23:23–24).

God is omnipotent. In our life, there is no situation or circumstances that He cannot transform. God is consistent and perfect in all that He does, Power, knowledge, wisdom, authority; He has everything in His hand. "… Jesus came to them and said, "All authority in heaven and on earth has been given to me" (Matthew 28:18). There is no one like our God!

God is Merciful

Regardless of our weaknesses or what we have done, God continues to show compassion and mercy towards us. He is man and God; He can relate to human kind and show us everlasting kindness. Because of His mercy we can still stand another day with hope in our hearts, desire and will to conquer fear. We are no longer defining by our mistakes but by His grace and mercy.

We have so many super heroes and role models that we all enjoy impersonating in our day to day life by dressing or talking like them. Most of those superheroes have weaknesses, flaws, something that they are afraid of or something they are unable to do. However, God is the only One who does not have any weaknesses or fear because he dominates over all things. All things exist because of Who He is, He is the source of all lives. Hence, listening to Him and emulating Him can only lead us to the right path. It is time to ignore and turn back to the lies and counterfeit and to recognize that He is the original and there is power in His name. Young and old, all can access His Kingdom. More than ever following Him, be obedient to Him is our key to learning who we are, who He is in prayers and reading continuously His word.

5. Types of Prayers

The Word of God provides us with samples of prayers and many types of supplications. For instance, we find the first prayer in the Bible "...At that time people began calling upon the name of the Lord", (Genesis 4:26). Furthermore, it states "...pray in the Spirit on all occasions with all kinds of prayers and requests. The most important prayer of all is the one that glorifies God, a broken spirit; a broken and contrite heart. During His passage on earth, one of Jesus Christ disciples asks Him how to pray and he taught them how to pray. Prayer is important, and it is our way to express our joy, pains and praises to God. Sometimes prayer can also be a silence, subsequently we can listen to what He has to say to us.

The Bible gives us at least eight major types of prayers:

1) Prayer of faith, which is found in James 5:13-16

2) Prayer of agreement or corporate prayer found in Acts 2:42

3) Prayer of request, petition, or supplication found in Philippians 4:6

4) Prayer of thanksgiving found in Psalm 95:2-3

5) Prayer of worship found in Acts 13:2-3

6) Prayer of consecration or dedication found in Matthew 26:39

7) Prayer of intercession found in 1Timothy 2:1

8) Prayer in the Spirit found in 1 Corinthians 14:14-15

CHAPTER XIV
AUTHOR'S VISIONS & SHARED TESTIMONIES

1. Through a Confession of Faith

I am about to ask you to do something that you have done before or maybe that you have never done, a confession of faith. For one reason or another you chose to go back to your old ways and start believing that all is over. Alone, you have tried and failed after many attempts. However, today, I am asking you to change the way you look at things, and surprisingly you may discover something greater than all you have experienced before.

In Galatians 3: 22 it reads, "But Scripture has locked up everything under the control of sin, so that what was promised, being given through faith in Jesus Christ, might be given to those who believe." To witness, to live and to experience God, it is simply an acknowledgement of our sins and remembering who created us. Knowing who we are simplifies our lives. With so much going on around the world, we cannot afford, nor do we want to risk living without Jesus. Even though, you may want to delay this moment, remember that tomorrow is never promised but your tomorrow can start today, "If we confess our sins, he is faithful and just and will forgive us our sins and purify us from all unrighteousness" (1 John 1:9).

We have only required a simple prayer of faith and admission that Jesus Christ died on the cross, and by this sacrifice, we are free. Free to encounter Him, free to start a relationship with Him, free to surrender our lives to our creator, free to be what we have called to be: worshipers and conquerors. We have done the things that we have done because we did not know any better; *now that we know better, we can act better.* Because you have been set free and you are saved, you can start accessing the power, the authority, the anointing, and a better sense of your life where you are right now with those Words. "Lord, when I think about what I have done, where I have been, I know for sure that I am not worthy to come to you. However, your Word declares; to come as we are, and you have made provision when you sent your only son Jesus Christ to die on the cross for our sins; please forgive me, I need you. Because of the blood of Jesus Christ, I have gained free access and I'm asking you to save me right now where I am. By faith, I believe that Jesus Christ is the Lord, and through Him I will gain the eternal life. I believe He died and rose on the third day for me. Lord may your will be done in my life, and from this day on I know for sure that you are my only God and Savior". Amen!

Guess what? Just like that, you are no longer slave of sins; you have been set free. Free from the burden of yesterday. Free from bondage and chains, your chains are broken in His name. You have taken the first big step, and this is the most important period in your life, giving your life to Jesus, you're Savior. Your next phase is to find a church and get a good foundation of the Word, which is based on the Bible's teachings. Quite often fear can give us a false sense of security, it can cause us to avoid what life has to offer and stay in our comfort zones. Today, I am asking you to agree to be uncomfortable. Most of the time, fear holds us back, we become paralyzed and suddenly we forget that life is a precious gift that needs to be lived, and cherished. "For God has not given us a spirit of fear, but of power and of love and of a sound mind" (2 Timothy 1:7).

Statistics should not hinder us from living life. In contrast, we need to use those statistics and make an impact because *each one of us holds a piece of the puzzle*. Henceforth, we ought to be able to love and to be compassionate in our homes, our schools, at work, and wherever we may be. Thus, we can live with hope and faith that conquer it all. "A new command I give you: Love one another. As I have loved you, so you must love one another. By this, everyone will know that you are my disciples if you love one another" (John 13:34 -35). Hence, come and you will see what the Lord can do. "Taste and see that the Lord is good; blessed is the one who takes refuge in him" (Psalm 34:8).

My hope for you is to find refuge in the great I am. Many have money, fame, and all that the world could offer; yet they are feeling empty. The only way to be fulfilled and to live on this earth with a sense of purpose and hope relies only on the great I am, Jesus Christ. He is the key, the way, the light, the truth and the solution to our daily inquiries.

The Samaritan woman shared it so loudly, after having an encounter with Jesus stated, "Everyone who drinks this water will be thirsty again, but whoever drinks the water I give them will never thirst. Indeed, the water I give them will become in them a spring of water welling up to eternal life" (John 4:13). Don't you want to experience Him? You have tried so many other options and it seems none of them has been working or bringing you the hope and the peace you have been searching for. Today, the invitation is offered to you, don't you want to connect with Him?

Even after praying that prayer of repentance your mind still wonders if you will get that second chance to start over. Jesus Christ is the One who will forgive you day after day. Whenever you acknowledge your sins and come to Him, He won't disown you. He does not blame or abandon you no matter what you have done. He is the God of many chances. Also, when God forgives take the time to forgive yourself, it is important. The enemy will use your old ways, your past and wrong doings to make you feel worthless, don't let him. You are free!

Paul had an encounter with the Lord on the road of Damascus after killing thousands of Christians (Acts 9). Yet, when he met with God he was no longer the persecutors of Christians but one that has been touched and rescued. After that encounter with the Lord, Paul suddenly realized there is no one like God who can transform his mind and life. God completely forgets our sins and transgressions; He forgives us and gives us a new identity in Him. Hence, you may lose some friends, and certain things in the world, but you will have an eternal relationship with God. One of my acquaintances, Azid Mohamed stated *"Things don't just happen, things happen just"* (2018). Remember, whenever everyone else sees a mess, He sees a masterpiece. Others may see weakness, He sees strength. Your family members and people around you may think you are a lost cause, He is the Redeemer, He can make you whole again, He is the potter. As your creator, He knows what you are made of. His love is unconditional, reliable, beyond science and understanding.

The best gift you could ever give yourself is the eternal life; simply because your spiritual life is a priority and it matters, The Gospel of Mark 8:36-37 states "What good is it for someone to gain the whole world, yet forfeit their soul? Or what can anyone give in exchange for their soul"? If for one reason or another it never occurred to you to learn and to connect with Jesus Christ, I urge and encourage you all today to come and taste this water, that source that never dries up. You will never thirst again!

For those of you who think that God is just a myth and refuse to acknowledge His power and presence. I invite you to open your heart, to risk it all, to walk that extra mile, to leave your comfort zone and to allow yourself to have an encounter with Him. God is already inside of you, now turn on the switch. Speak; you will hear His voice hidden in your heart. Many of you are mad and refuse to understand how God can let His people suffer and He never dares to say a word. What kind of God can He be if poverty, war and destruction seem without an end? Where was God when your parents past away? Where was God when your life took the turn it took?

I invite you to have that communication with God as He stated "Come to me, all you who are weary and burdened, and I will give you rest. Take my yoke upon you and learn from me, for I am gentle and humble in heart, and you will find rest for your souls. For my yoke is easy and my burden is light" (Matthew 11: 28 -30).

2. Powerful Testimonies

Do we really know "That all things work together for good to them that love God, to them who are the called according to his purpose?" Angela Leite reported that she had memorized and recited this verse numerous times before. Nevertheless, in 2004 this verse had a total different meaning for her. As anyone, she could not understand how a series of trials that were coming toward her family's life and hers could in any way be good.

In 2001, her husband who is a minister of the gospel, accepted a call to leave a structured and growing church and they packed their bags and crossed the Atlantic heading toward the Cape Verde Islands. They knew that God had great things for them there, and they were willing to obey His call. During the time that they stayed there, they built a place where they could feed daily more than one hundred children, teach in the theological school, and pastor a Church. It was a tough decision but after praying and crying unto the Lord for a long time, she and her husband decided to return to the United States. It was some type of confirmation when God opened doors and allowed her to go back to her old position in the public schools. Taking advantage of the health insurance, she decided to submit to a complete checkup, something she had not done for years. That's when the biggest storm in their lives started. After making a mammogram, the doctors discovered a malignant tumor in her left breast. It was an invasive cancer that needed to be treated immediately. Two days after the biopsy she had a bilateral mastectomy with simultaneous reconstruction. At first, she thought that it was the best idea the disease would be removed for good, and she would still have breasts, which are for any woman, part of her femininity. However, it did not happen as planned.

Her husband and her private nurse, were the ones who would bathe, do the bandages, and support her. One day, her husband noticed that the appearance of her breast was not normal and decided to bring her to the surgeon. In fact, something was wrong. Her body had rejected the implants, and she was taken to the operation room to remove the necropsy skin. The problem was that the infection had already spread to other parts of her body. For about twenty-one days, she was hooked on machines, wires everywhere, tubes connected to buckets that would remove all the contamination. She was taken to the operation room for about thirteen times. After many treatments, countless chemotherapy and radiation treatments, and going back and forth to the hospital. In 2004, a team of doctors called Angela's husband and stated, "We have done all that we can, we used all the resources and technologies available to us and we are sorry; there is nothing else that we can do for you. It is over.

What do you do when the people who have the knowledge to help you are powerless and unable? After hearing those Words, her husband responded, "Great! I am happy to hear that you have done all you can; that is good news. Thank you." Intrigued and confused, the doctors thought he was in denial or insane. Who in his or her right mind replies that it is good news to hear those death-sentence Words? With an empty and painful heart, Angela and her husband gathered their belongings from the hospital, but their soul and faith bounced back, and as they reached their destination, they went to the One from whom all blessings flow; they went back to the source of all things, Jesus Christ.

Instead of being isolated, depressed, desperate and in despair, Angela's husband contacted all the saints that he knew here in the United States, in Brazil and in Cape Verde. They contacted family members all over the world and started to bring their case to the Lord in prayer. From that moment, they remembered whose they are, and they reached out to all believers and people of faith to intercede, believers who truly accept as true that His name is Jehovah Rapha; God our healer. He is the one who can still perform miracles. With one heart, one spirit and one goal to pray for recovery, Angela reported that she could feel in her body and spirit the answer to their prayers. Despite all this suffering, she knew that the God that she serves was by her side and if He wanted, He would keep her alive.

During her personal time of prayer, Angela stated that every time she had to be submitted to treatment and knew it could be the end of her life, she had this specific prayer, "*Lord, I am in your hands; I understand that this (treatment, surgery, procedure) can be fatal. I belong to you. Your plans for my life are greater than mine. If it is your desire that I die, I want to be prepared but if you have something else for me, I want to obey you.*" Moreover, during her personal time of prayer, Angela stated, "*Lord, if it is not my time yet, I am asking you to heal me. The doctor said it is over. However, I know that you can replace those cancerous cells into new and rejuvenated ones but if it is my time, may your will be done. Should you agree to spare my life from this disease, I want to be where you want me to be, I want to go wherever you lead me and share with the world how powerful and caring our God is.*"

Going through the treatment meant to be submitted to chemotherapy and radiation. She lost all her hair and lost weight. She lost her two breasts, but she gained the faith that transport mountains. Our God is powerful to make much more than what we can think or ask for, To Him all the glory. Thirteen years have passed; she is here to testify of this wonderful God: "He is the God of impossible things. Now, I know that "all things work together for good". I am a miracle of God, and I know that He kept me alive to testify about it". When I told Angela that I was writing a book and that I would like to share her testimonial, she said, "please, go ahead, please do."

Her story can uplift others. I am not sure who wanted to learn about her story, but this testimony is for all of us. Our God is still in the business of doing the unheard and the unseen, if we only keep up the faith and surrender all to Him in prayers! Angela realized that her life has a purpose; hence, she has decided to take an early retirement and go back to her homeland to preach, to support, to motivate and preach the Gospel that Jesus Christ is the Lord, the Healer and the Way.

Here is another testimony that will inspire and remind all of us that we cannot afford to lose hope or live life through fear. The gift of discernment is essential in any Christian's life. Our God is awesome, and He continues to operate miracles in our daily life.

Her name is Owepatrice Gaillard. She has no significant past medical history. Her father deceased from end-stage renal disease and was on dialysis, and her mother is alive but has a history of a heart condition. Late in 2014, she felt the urge to increase the value of her life insurance, so she called her agent to start the process. The process to modify the insurance policy included a physical exam; it was during this exam that they identified that her urine protein levels were off the charts. She was completely asymptomatic and was feeling great. To follow through, she made an appointment with her physician to verify the findings; it was at that appointment that the physician diagnosed her with a complex disease; lupus. The doctor also ordered a kidney biopsy to confirm. Subsequently to this physician appointment, she began to develop swelling of both legs to the point where she could not wear shoes. Once the kidney biopsy results confirmed the diagnosis of lupus, the nephrologist and the rheumatologist started treatment, consisting of multiple oral medications and injections. She was on a total of seven different oral medications several times daily and an injection twice a week. In addition to blood work every thirty days, she must see several physicians to make sure the side effects of the medications did not destroy her other organs.

She had to see a cardiologist to monitor her heart, an eye specialist to monitor the health of her eyes, and a dermatologist to treat her skin conditions that she developed because of the disease process. She also required a bone scan to monitor her bones and water aspirated from her knee joints due to massive swelling. Due to the high doses of prednisone she had to take, her skin began to thin out and she began losing her hair. During this process, she was placed on short-term disability by her physician and issued a handicap sticker for her car. It became very taxing for her to walk long distances; her legs would become very weak and unable to hold her body weight. Her kidney function was consistently dropping, and when she reached 60 percent kidney function, the nephrologist stated that if she continued to drop, she would need to begin dialysis treatments.

The word dialysis made her remember her dad and immediately it all made sense, and she understood that she was under attack by a generational curse. Therefore, knowing that what is flesh is flesh, and what is spirit is spirit, she knew the medications could not help her and that the medications made her worse. At that point she decided to stop the medications, started vitamins, trusted God and went into spiritual warfare. She held off seeing her doctors for a few months and just persisted in prayers and warfare with back up by her church sisters.

After a few months, when she finally felt peace in her spirit, somehow, she knew God had done it. Henceforth, she scheduled an appointment to see her nephrologist and completed the necessary blood work before each appointment. It was at that appointment in late December of 2015 that her blood work would show improvement up to 80 percent. She took authority and started to speak to her body telling it that *"I was not created with eighty percent kidney function, and I command you to rise-up to one hundred percent function as it was in the beginning."* Her prayer reminded me of so many saints. Especially Elijah, who was a human being who prayed earnestly that it would not rain, and it did not rain.

Her church sisters agreed with her at a miracle night-prayer meeting that they had at church once a month. In early February of 2016, she returned to the nephrologist after the result of her lab work is completed. The doctor reported that her kidney was improved to 90 percent. She repeated the cycle of warfare and went back to miracle night prayer at church, where her sisters laid hands on her and commanded the kidneys to rise to 100 percent. It was at the very last appointment in March of 2016 that the doctor would be amazed when he saw the blood results showing her kidneys were up to 120 percent function without the medications. That is what amazed the doctor even more because she told him at that visit that she had stopped the medications months before. "In Christ alone, I no longer need a disabled handicap sticker for my car because I am well in Jesus name," she said. Glory to God and Amen!

Even though the Word of God is effective and food to our soul, unfortunately, some of us are afraid to ask. Many of us are fearful to be rejected and countless times we do not ask because we are ashamed. Notice that there is no shame in asking and even the Word of God teaches us that if we ask, we shall receive. "So, I say to you: Ask and it will be given to you; seek and you will find; knock and the door will be opened to you. For everyone who asks receives; the one who seeks finds; and to the one who knocks, the door will be opened" (Luke 11:9-10). Living on this earth is not easy, that is why we need to depend on God and to bring our burdens to Him. He also reminded us that we have an enemy and this adversary is vicious, the only way we can resist is by holding on to faith, "Be sober, be vigilant, because your adversary the devil walketh about as a roaring lion, seeking whom he may devour" (1 Peter 5:8).

One of the things that we have learned, God answers always. He is always on time. We may not get the expected answer that we wished for, but His timing never failed. Where we stand when trouble knocks on our doors can be de the determining factor between our fear or our faith. Matthew 16:24 -26 "Take Up Your Cross and Follow Jesus. Then Jesus told his disciples, "If anyone would come after me, let him deny himself and take up his cross and follow me. For whoever would save his life will lose it, but whoever loses his life for my sake will find it. For what will it profit a man if he gains the whole world and forfeits his soul? Or what shall a man give in return for his soul?

While I shared these testimonies of faith and total surrender with so much passion and commitment to the Word and will of God in the lives of my sisters. I would be remiss not to present other ways that God answered to His faithful servants. Believers ought to know the ultimate plan God has for us is always good. I have had the unique honor and privilege to connect and commune with some men and women of faith. For them, God's answer, my grace is sufficient for you, for my power is made perfect in weakness (2 Corinthians 12:9 b), or welcome home my child! As the disciple Paul stated in 2 Timothy 4: 7 "I have fought the good fight, I have finished the race, I have kept the faith".

3. Faithful till the end. Homage to the late Dr. Joseph Mona!

One day, while visiting my mother, she introduced me to a person and stated; "You see this woman here; she has been praying for you." I smiled, gave her a kiss and said, "Thank you for devoting time to pray for my family." Humbly she responded, "It is my duty!" That introduction was a brief one, until I had the distinct honor to meet her again at a mutual friend's house. That day, we spend hours talking about miraculous things that God has done in our lives, how serious she is when it comes to praying for people. We did not even realize that the people we were visiting were gone. From that day on, the beginning of a loving and healthy relationship was born. Our conversation about life, love, relationship, the Word of God, respect and faith never ended.

Three years ago, during the month of April or the month of May I was asked to share a Word via a prayer line. I am not a preacher; however, I believe that anyone who has an encounter with the Lord can share and testify who the Lord is in their lives and what He has done for them. Due to a prior commitment, I was driving when it was time to share a Word with the group. I am thankful for Bluetooth technology that enables me to drive safely without holding the phone. I was led to share a passage in the Bible that I have learned and read over and over when life throws its challenges at me. This passage reaffirms the truth that I am not and will never be alone. Isaiah 43: 2 "When you pass through the waters, I will be with you;

and when you pass through the rivers, they will not sweep over you. When you walk through the fire, you will not be burned; the flames will not set you ablaze". The following day, I received a call from that same lady who became my dear best friend, my go to person, my classmate, my mentor, more importantly, my spiritual mother. Her name was Marie Mona Joseph; however, I called her Mo because she was my Mo, my Mojo.

Henceforth, it was logical when I received a call from her the following day just to check in. After she made sure that I and the family were doing fine. She proceeded by saying how she was listening to me on the prayer line and heard the Word that I shared. She reported how the message made her feel and believed to her core that message was especially for her and that Word did something in her spirit a way she never experienced before. I responded, "I wonder if God is not talking to me too Mo?" She boldly said, in a way that she can only talk, as though she was singing and dancing, in a serious deep voice, "Soraya, oh no, the way that I felt that day, the message was truly mine and I thank my Daddy because He made provisions and reassured me that I am not alone". Amen, I replied also and declared forfeit. In some strange way, I knew that she may be right; but who could ever tell. Yes, God was preparing us for something greater.

It was late in August of 2016, that my best friend, my sister, my prayer warrior was diagnosed with stage four cancer. Boldly, with a smile on her face, she told the doctors, really? Ok, so what are we working with? As a nurse, herself, she knew what stage four cancer meant and the fact that it already spread in her body, she knew what she was dealing with. However, as a servant of God, she declares authority and stated, "Soraya we are going to beat this cancer in the name of Jesus and she started to declare the Words of hope, faith and complete surrender to God's will in her life. She was ready to come back to our TV show "The Zone" to share with whomever what cancer is and what it looks like as she was accustomed to share her knowledge when it comes to health. The mental, spiritual health, the life of people mattered to her, more importantly their relationship with one another and God was even greater.

As she was battling that vicious disease, never did her faith waver. In fact, she was finishing her doctorate degree in Christian Counseling and she was able to reach the deadline for graduation. She only had one week to live when she sent me her last text that read "I miss you more. I have great news for us. I love you and I am happy for you. I miss getting better, I am tired, no…" When I finally had a chance to see her, she was weak in her body but strong in faith. She was ready to see Daddy; she was ready to leave this earth with a smile on her face and still believing that she is not alone. I had the distinct honor to know Dr. Mo. More importantly, to enjoy a tête-à-tête about the unconditional love of God for us in good or bad times. I was privileged to witness faith that is rooted in God's Word and nothing in this world, not even cancer could take it away. Dr. Mo passed on June 8th, 2017 but her legacy of love, prayer, and faith is forever engraved in my daily walk with God.

To her tribute, I shared "As the sun shines in the morning, your sun rays are felt and enlightened my world. You open a door that is full of great memories; time of prayers, songs, dances, jokes, stories and babysitting time that are engraved in my mind and soul. I'll continue to carry on your spirit of hope, support, faith, and dedication to the Word of God. I enjoyed our unique journey of faith, miraculous grace, & love. Thanks, Dr. Mo, I love you!

We must be vigilant and be aware of the battle. Yet, understand the battle has already been won on the cross by our Savior, Jesus Christ. Therefore, we can still use the Words of Job "Naked I came from my mother's womb, and naked I will depart. The Lord gave, and the Lord has taken away; may the name of the Lord be praised" (Job 1:21). Sometimes the answer may not be healing; it can also be it is time to come to your Daddy!

3. Now what?

What is stopping us from making our voices heard is still unknown. We have the Word; the Holy Spirit and it seems that everyone is busy while people are dying. "My people are destroyed for lack of knowledge…Because you have rejected knowledge, I also will reject you from being priest for me because you have forgotten the law of your God, I also will forget your children" (Hosea 4:6). The world is in desperate need of hope and salvation; their cries are heard and not ignored, but believers are singing songs of courage and deliverance, and no one seems to pay attention. God is kind and understanding toward our weaknesses, but He requires us to go forward in faith, and the Bible is clear that faith does not mature and strengthen without trials. Hence, before you start thinking about your flaws and all the challenges ahead, you should first think about your blessings. The Word of God is important; it is the only source of salvation and that salvation is only through faith. Yes, the unknown is never uncertain with God. You cannot try God's solution to be ashamed. "Blessed are those whose strength is in you, whose hearts are set on pilgrimage" (Psalm 84:5). The things of the world may seem the best to have; however, the best is always in God; we have it all to win and nothing to lose.

Adversity is the most effective tool to develop a strong faith. Adversity also builds character. That pattern is evident in Scripture. God takes each one of us through fearful situations, and as we learn to obey God's Word and allow it to saturate our thoughts, we find each trial becomes a stepping stone to a stronger and deeper faith. It gives us that ability to say, "He sustained me in the past, He'll carry me through today, and

121

He'll uphold me in the future!" God worked this way in David's life. When David volunteered to fight against Goliath, he said, "The Lord who delivered me from the paw of the lion and the paw of the bear will deliver me from the hand of this Philistine" (1 Samuel 17:37). David knew the God who had sustained him through dangerous situations in the past. He had seen and experienced God's power and protection in his life, and this developed within him a fearless faith. David displayed a faith in the ways that he worshiped and praised God for His name and what He had done in His life, a thankful heart. Furthermore, the way David humbled himself, the trust, reverence, and respect He had for the Lord are excellent quality that we should imitate as true believers.

The Word of God is rich with promises for us to hold on to and to claim for ourselves. When we face financial trouble, the Bible tells us, "And my God will supply all your needs according to His riches in glory in Christ Jesus" (Philippians 4:19). If we are anxious about a future decision, the Bible reminds us that God will "instruct you and teach you in the way you should go; I will counsel you with my eye upon you" (Psalm 32:8). In sickness, trials and tribulations, we can remember that Romans 5:3-5 says, "Not only so, but we also glory in our sufferings, because we know that suffering produces perseverance; perseverance, character; and character, hope. And hope does not put us to shame, because God's love has been poured out into our hearts through the Holy Spirit, who has been given to us." If someone turns against us, we can be comforted by the Words in Romans 8:31, "If God is for us who can be against us!"

Throughout life we will continue to face various trials that would cause doubts and fear, but God assures us that we can know a calm peace through every situation, "And the peace of God, which transcends all understanding, will guard your hearts and your minds in Christ Jesus" (Philippians 4:7). More importantly, when we accept, acknowledge, understand, and receive the Word of God in His powerful being; we can summarize, "The righteous person will live by his faithfulness" (Habakkuk 2:4).

As we have seen throughout the Word of God, the faith that conquers fear is a faith that is anchored in the Word of God. We have seen an antagonistic relationship between faith and fear, for where there is faith, fear cannot reside. It is either one or the other. Which one do you choose? When you are facing adversity and trials in your life? One cannot have faith and live in fear, it is impossible. Fear and faith cannot coexist. We are quite familiar with the stories of Abraham, Joseph, Daniel, and Job. Hence, what is our story and position for the next generation? Those powerful testimonies from Angela, Owepatrice, and all the saints should be a reminder of God's word "so is my word that goes out from my mouth: It will not return to me empty but will accomplish what I desire and achieve the purpose for which I sent it (Isiah 55:11).

Those believers found themselves in difficult situations while the enemy attempted to discourage and even kill them, but they did not allow fear of disease, the unknown, natural disaster, isolation or death stop them from obeying and submitting to God. They trusted their God to see them through and to live a victorious life because they knew who they are. Adversities, trials, and tribulations are fragment of everyday life. As we have seen in the news, terror is rampant. Killing and destruction are chunk of everyday life. We, believers and society, have a decision to make and we have a responsibility. We could either live in fear, hide out or we can choose to believe in God and walk by faith. The decision to trust, to obey God, and believe that He is ready, willing and able to guide and protect us in all circumstances. Faith is a necessity, for without faith it is impossible to live in this lost world. Conquering our fears is a day-to-day task even though it is daunting at best. Additionally, we are unable to please God if we do not have faith. It is my hope and prayer that those who take the time to read this book will ask themselves the following questions:

> Am I where I'm supposed to be with God?
> What is it that I fear the most? And why?
> Can I afford not to jump the leap of faith?
> How long are you willing to stay stuck in a cage?
> When are you going to step out and break free?
> Does my life reflect God's character and attributes?
> What is stopping me from facing my fear?
> What is preventing me from worshiping God?
> Am I ready to live in faith and not by sight?
> What are my talents?
> When and how am I going to use my talents for God?
> What should I do to solidify or strengthen my relationship with God?
> And finally, is there anyone around me in my circle of friends who may need an encounter with God?

Regardless of the answers to those questions, today you have been giving wings to fly; wings that have always been with you since birth, however fear disabled you to access them. You have received a powerful tool that will make your existence on this earth count. You are stronger than you have ever imagined. Yes, believe it; you are ready to make an impact and seal the deed of your hope and security. You will no longer live that unbalanced and double minded life in any form or shape when fears come your way. It is time to say good bye fear, do not come back, it is over! Currently, the antidote has been given to you. Faith to succeed, faith to no longer be a slave of sins, faith to grasp the reality of your root, faith to seek for more in His presence, faith to live as a conqueror, faith that your situation is not permanent but temporary, faith that transcend the doubts, faith to break loose, faith to see the sun that rises, and the rainbows of colors in period of a gray sky. Faith, beyond understanding!

"For God has not given us a spirit of fear, but of power and of love and of a sound mind" (1 Timothy 1: 7). You will live by faith and no longer by the unfounded lies of the enemy. You are called conqueror, hopeful, blessed, chosen, anointed, gifted and faithful. Respond to your new name, walk with your head up, be proud, be bold in declaring "The Lord is my shepherd; I shall not want. He makes me to lie down in green pastures; He leads me beside the still waters. He restores my soul; He leads me in the paths of righteousness For His name's sake. Yea, though I walk through the valley of the shadow of death, I will fear no evil, for you are with me, your rod and your staff, they comfort me. You prepare a table before me in the presence of my enemies, you anoint my head with oil, and my cup runs over. Surely goodness and mercy shall follow me All the days of my life, and I will dwell in the house of the Lord Forever" (Psalms 23).

Our faith polishes and shines sunnier when difficult times, prosecutions cross our paths. We may not feel like shouting, dancing praying when we are face with those challenges. However, we must always remember who we are in Christ and His word. He conquered it all; in Him we are more than a conqueror. More than ever, it is time to break that unhealthy relationship with fear. Throughout my journey with the Lord I conclude, while the enemy is trying to destroy our lives, our relationships, our children, our schools, our health, our homes, our countries, our spouses, our work environment or even our place of worship, just remember; God has already made provisions! May you find comfort and peace, because sooner or later, you will overcome those challenges in your life. Fear cannot stop you anymore, this relationship is over. You were born to dominate over all things on the earth.

"The enemy is doing something; God has already done everything".
(Présumé Calixte, 2018)

5. Your Personal Notes:

....

....

....

....

....

....

....

....

....

....

....

....

....

....

....

No matter what it is that you are facing in your life right now; please, hold on tight. This period is not permanent but temporary. You are not alone, you are truly loved beyond your wildest imagination. Have faith and keep on believing.

References

Bevere, J. (2006). *The Fear of the Lord Discover the Key to Intimately Knowing God*. Lake Mary, FL: Charisma House.

Brezsny, Rob. (2009). *Pronoia Is the Antidote for Paranoia: How the Whole World Is Conspiring to Shower You with Blessings*. Berkeley, CA: North Atlantic Books.

Dweck, C. S. (2006). *Mindset: The New Psychology of Success*. New York: Random House.

Gill, A. L. (1999), *GOD'S PROMISES for Your Every Need*, Nashville, TN: Thomas Nelson Inc.

Hanh, N. (2013). *Fear: Essential Wisdom for Getting through the Storm*. London: HarperCollins Publisher.

Hawkins, L. J. (2015). *When a Man Finds a Wife: Should I Wait for Him to Find Me or Catch Him while I Can?* Bloomington, IN: I Universe.

Evans, A. R. (1999). *The Healing Church: Practical Programs for Health Ministries*. Cleveland: The Pilgrim Press / United Church Press.

Jeremiah, D. (1997), *Prayer, the Great Adventure*. Sisters, OR: Multnomah Publisher Inc.

Kübler-Ross, E. (1997). *On Death and Dying: What the Dying Have to Teach Doctors, Nurses, Clergy and Their Own Families*. Montgomery, AL: Life A profound lesson for the living.

Meyer, J. (1996) *Filled with the Spirit, Understanding God's Power in Your Life*, New York: Faith Works.

Newbell, Trillia J. (2013). *Fear and Faith: Finding the Peace Your Heart Craves.* Chicago: Moody Press.

Raley, J., and D. Raley (2013), *The Word for You Today, Strength and Guidance for Daily Living.* Ormond Beach, FL: Calvary Christian Center.

Ross, J. (2009). *Triumph over Fear: A Book of Help and Hope for People with Anxiety, Panic Attacks, and Phobias.* New York: Bantam Books.

Schaub, R. and B. J. Schaub (2009), *The End of Fear. A Spiritual Path for Realists*, New York: Hay House Inc.

Saillens, R. (2006). *Le Mystère de la Foi. Exposé évangélique d'après Les Saintes Écritures.* Nogent-sur-Marne, France : Association Auxiliaire de l'Institut Biblique.

Sisgold, Steve. (2011). *Conscious and Unconscious Regression: Discovering and Reliving Earlier Experiences that May Influence How You Behave Now.*

Walker, A. (2016). "Voice out Gun Apologists: Terrorist Attack Must Spark Unity, Not Finger-pointing." *The Boston Globe*, June 12, 2016. Accessed on June 22, 2016.

Youssef, M. (2015), *Faith Conquers Fear: My Journal Leading the Way*, Atlanta, GA Leading the Way.

Young, S. (2004), *Devotions for Every Day of the Year. Jesus Calling, Enjoying Peace in His Presence*, Nashville, TN: Thomas Nelson.

List of websites:

http://www.ambiancefm.com/

https://www.biblegateway

http://drleaf.com/about/toxic-thoughts

http://www.biography.com/people/elisabeth-kubler-ross-262762

http://www.bible-history.com/faussets/F/Faith/

http://www.bustle.com/articles/125608-what-does-isis-mean-some-of-the-terrorist-groups-names-are-more-controversial-than-others (ISIS) MEANING

https://www.ibelieve.com/health-beauty/30-day-prayer-challenge-fighting-fear-and-anxiety-with-the-promises-of-god.html

https://www.google.com/search?q=fear+is+a+liar&rlz=1C1OPRA_enUS543US543&oq=fear+is+a+liar&aqs=chrome.69i57j69i59.2729j0j7&sourceid=chrome&ie=UTF-8

http://time.com/4290861/checking-account-money-mood/?xid=newsletter-brief.

http://christianity.about.com/od/newchristians/qt/healthyfaith12.htm

http://time.com/4290861/checking-account-money-mood/?xid=newsletter-brief.

http://christianity.about.com/od/newchristians/qt/healthyfaith12.htm

https://4mygodsglory.Wordpress.com/2013/11/05/i-am-a-christian-maya-angelou/

http://www.history.com/topics/galileo-galilei

http://www.merriam-webster.com/dictionary/faith

http://www. mentalhealthamerica.net

http://www.ministryofthesentinels.org/

https://www.psychologytoday.com/blog/life-in-body/201409/conscious-and-unconscious-regression"

http://www.spacesupport.org

https://www.ziglar.com/quotes/your-attitude-not-your-aptitude/

Info & Support:

Ambiance FM; Jacmel (617) 820 0848

GabyJo Entertainment

Radio Télé Ambiance, Jacmel Zone Paskét

Soraya Media Group Inc.

Spacesupport.org

The Zone Show, Boston/ Brockton